Helping Low Achievers Succeed at Mathematics

SPRINGBOARDS FOR TEACHING

Helping Low Achievers Succeed at Mathematics

Derek Haylock
Marcel D'Eon

Trifolium Books Inc.
Fitzhenry & Whiteside
TORONTO, CANADA

Trifolium Books Inc.
a Fitzhenry & Whiteside Company
195 Allstate Parkway,
Markham, Ontario L3R 4T8

In the Unites States
Fitzhenry & Whiteside Limited
121 Harvard Avenue, Suite 2
Allston, Massachusetts 02134

www.fitzhenry.ca   godwit@fitzhenry.ca

Authorized adaptation based on the original edition published by Paul Chapman Publishing Ltd.: Teaching Mathematics to Low Attainers 8-12 ©1991 Derek Haylock.

Canadian Cataloguing in Publication Data

Haylock, Derek
    Helping low achievers succeed at mathematics: grade 2-8

(Springboards for teaching)
Includes bibliographical references and index.
ISBN 1-55244-010-9

1.   Mathematics – Study and teaching (Elementary). 2. Underachievers
I. D'Eon, Marcel F., 1953—   .II. Title III. Series

QA135.5.H417 1999   372.7'044   C99-931595-1

Project Editor: Rosemary Tanner
Design, layout original graphics: Heidy Lawrance Associates
Cover design: Kerry Designs

Printed and bound in Canada
10 9 8 7 6 5 4 3 2

Fitzhenry & Whiteside acknowledges with thanks the Canada Council for the Arts, the Government of Canada through its Book Publishing Industry Development Program, and the Ontario Arts Council for their support in our publishing program.

TABLE OF CONTENTS

Acknowledgments

The publishers and authors would like to thank the many educators and associates who took the time to provide valuable reviews, in particular, Trevor Brown of the Toronto District School Board, Lee McMenemy of the Algoma District School Board, Ann Louise Revells of the Ottawa-Carleton Catholic District School Board, Liliane Gauthier of Saskatchewan Education, Sheryl Mills of Mills Consulting, and Janelle Phillips, now retired from the Saskatoon Board of Education.

Dedication

*We would like to dedicate this book to those teachers, parents,
teacher associates and administrators who work with our children to
help them unravel the mystery of mathematics, and to
those students who find mathematics a struggle to master.*

Introduction

Have you ever had the wonderful experience of seeing students' enthusiasm as they connect real-world situations to the concepts you have taught them? Derek Haylock relates one such experience in which he and a teacher working together helped students connect a supermarket activity dealing with money to the measurement tasks before them. These students were bursting to tell the teacher that they knew what operation to enter on their calculators to answer the questions that had been posed. What made their enthusiasm so wonderful was the fact that these were children who did not usually experience success in mathematics. For them, understanding was a rare experience. Suddenly, in the middle of all this excited activity, the school bell rang to signal the end of the lesson. As if on cue, the whole class spontaneously groaned!

This story expresses what we hope to accomplish by writing this book. We have the same ends in mind that you do, especially for low-achieving students. Our goal is to turn failure and frustration with mathematics into success and excitement. Derek, a mathematics educator in the UK, wrote about his ideas for helping these students in the early 1990s. Marcel D'Eon, a Canadian mathematics educator, has built upon Derek's experience, adding his own North American perspective, as well as ideas that have come from his own work. Packed with practical activities and insights, we hope this book will give you ideas to help your low achieving students grow in mathematical understanding and competency so you, too, can be part of the excitement!

Features of this book

This book is for teachers, parents, those who home-school, principals, and teacher associates who are concerned about and involved in helping low-achieving students learn mathematics. Chapter 1 outlines who our low achievers are. Chapter 2 gives a brief overview of a theory of teaching mathematics in order to justify our approach with low achievers. Chapter 3 explores the question: why can math be such a difficult subject for many students to learn? We discuss answers based on the nature of the discipline and the way math is often taught in school. Each chapter that follows gives an approach to teaching mathematics in specific areas with detailed suggestions, activities, and learning tasks.

Topics include place value, measurement, numerical operations, fractions, and working with money. For an in-depth treatment of concepts and principles in elementary school mathematics, readers are directed to the Resources section at the back. *Mathematics Every Elementary Teacher Should Know — Grades K–8 ©1999*, a new Trifolium title by Derek Haylock and Doug McDougall, deals comprehensively with the topic. Our focus in this book is on specific practical approaches to helping low-achieving students learn mathematics.

Teaching mathematics to low-achieving students

Teaching mathematics to low achievers in Grades 2–8 is one of the most challenging jobs in the world. Teachers will not argue with us when we assert that teaching is one of the hardest professions that anyone could enter. Most elementary and junior high school teachers are required to cover the whole spectrum of subjects for students whose range of competence is gradually becoming more diverse. Mathematics is often the subject that is most worrying for many teachers. And, judging by our conversations with many teachers, teaching those who do not do well at the subject is particularly demanding.

Most of Derek Haylock's experience with low-achieving students was gained in the middle schools of Norfolk, England. For a number of years, he regularly spent time teaching various groups of low achievers in mathematics or worked alongside and consulted with their teachers. For two years at the University of East Anglia, he directed a project entitled "Using Calculators to Aid Numeracy," in which a dozen local teachers worked with him on curriculum development in mathematics. This book derives directly from his personal experience of low-achieving students, their difficulties and achievements, and the problems encountered by their teachers.

Marcel D'Eon taught mathematics at the elementary school level for mixed ability groups, low-achieving students; and academically talented children for 16 years. He has also delivered in-service sessions for practicing teachers and taught prospective teachers at the University of Saskatchewan, Saskatoon, Canada. He was on the reference committee for a provincial, middle-years curriculum revision and participated in a local school division's mathematics curriculum revision project. His approach has always been very pragmatic — using any method that might help his students learn mathematics with understanding, particularly those who were struggling.

This book does not purport to be either comprehensive or definitive. It describes simply what our personal research and experiences led us to think about the nature of the problems facing low-achieving students and their teachers. We have presented what we consider to be the best strategies for tackling these problems, and what might constitute an appropriate curriculum. We have included many suggestions for activities which have been tried with various groups of students and which seem to have great potential for helping them. We have tried to write a book that is useful to teachers, parents, and others who want to help students whose progress in mathematics compares unfavorably with that of their contemporaries. We hope that you find it useful in helping students develop a much greater sense of achievement in mathematics and a solid foundation for future successes.

The Authors

Who Are Our Low Achievers?

FEATURES OF THIS CHAPTER

- a list of frequently encountered characteristics of low achievers
- a brief description of some factors related to low achievement in school mathematics
- some common labels applied to low achievers

Some characteristics of low achievers in mathematics

In a survey involving some 215 Grade 5 school children, their teachers were asked to consider a list of statements which referred to various factors often associated with low achievement in mathematics (Haylock, 1986). For each child with a score in the bottom 20% on a standardized mathematics test, the teachers were asked to indicate whether, in their judgment, the statements provided described the child. The 22 statements were based on possible factors associated with low achievement in mathematics found in previous studies, such as those by Ross (1964), Lumb (1978), and Denvir et al. (1982). The five most selected statements are listed below, along with their frequency of selection. The remaining 17 statements have not been listed as they applied to 45% or fewer of the low-achieving mathematics students.

- has been considered low achieving in mathematics from the first year in this school (82%)
- is low achieving in most areas of the curriculum (79%)
- has poorly developed reading skills (77%)
- is equally poor in all aspects of mathematics (74%)
- has poorly developed language skills (70%)

Early identification and proper intervention can make a noticeable difference in the lives of low achievers.

Several significant points emerge from this survey. First of all, the statement at the top of the list suggests that students can be identified as low achievers in mathematics by the age of 8 (Grade 3), if not earlier, and often remain in this category throughout the upper elementary years. This lends some support to our view that these are the crucial years for tackling the problems of these students. There is evidence to suggest that many of the mathematical tasks at which low-achieving students fail around the age of 12 will still be beyond them when they leave secondary school (Hart, 1981). So, if by Grade 3 we can confidently identify students who have particular problems in mathematics, then we should surely be able to design an appropriate curriculum for these students from that age onward, and not just subject them to exactly the same mathematical diet as that provided for average and above-average students. Furthermore, recent research on the relationship between mathematics achievement and both self-concept and self-efficacy (self-efficacy is the more specific belief in ability) has emphasized the importance of success for students (Jackson & Canada, 1995; Pajares & Miller, 1994). Beliefs about mathematics and about one's abilities to do math have a strong influence on success (and vice versa). We can do our students a great service by providing them with appropriate instruction that leads to success.

Factors related to low achievement in mathematics

Several factors contribute to the difficulties which low achievers have in learning mathematics. Some of these are root causes (e.g., reading problems) and some are consequences as well as cause (e.g., mathematics anxiety). It is important for the teacher to be aware of these factors in order to better understand the students and thereby help them succeed.

Reading and language problems

Use alternative ways of giving directions in mathematics, rather than relying heavily on only one form of communication.

Poor reading and language skills are frequently associated with low achievement in mathematics. In the survey quoted above, this was true for about three-quarters of the children sampled. Also, low-achieving boys have poorly developed reading skills significantly more frequently than low-achieving girls.

This reinforces the points about the particular difficulties associated with the complex language structures of mathematics. But it also underlines how *inappropriate* it would be to use any teaching method which relies heavily on the written word as the medium for instruction in mathematics. One study of children's errors in written mathematical tasks (Clement, 1980) found that 24% of the errors made by low-achieving 12-year-olds were simply reading or comprehension errors. The sheer cognitive strain of reading the instructions for the task makes it most unlikely that they will comprehend the mathematics. Derek recalls a typical conversation he had with one student who was struggling with an activity card and called for assistance.

"What's the problem?"

"I don't understand what I have to do."

"What does the card say then?"

(Hesitatingly) "Draw a square . . . with side ten centimeters . . . and divide it into five equal parts."

"So, what's the problem?"

"What do I have to do?"

"You have to draw a square with side ten centimeters and divide it into five equal parts."

"Oh, I see!" (Proceeds to do it)

The extraordinary point about this conversation is that all Derek did was to repeat back to the student exactly what he had read, and yet because he was hearing it rather than reading it, he was able to understand what was required mathematically.

Perceptual problems

Success in many mathematical tasks requires confident handling of basic spatial concepts such as left, right, above, below, over, and under. Intellectual challenges of this kind show up in reversals of figures and confusions between, for example, 14 and 41. Certain mathematical processes are particularly difficult for some children because they involve a right-to-left movement, such as starting with the units when doing addition and subtraction set out in vertical form, contrary to the standard left-to-right movement which is reinforced in reading. Teachers can have students pair up and check each other to avoid making these kinds of perceptual errors.

> Teachers can help students by teaching them to check their perceptions with another student or the teacher.

Attention Deficit Disorder

Children with attention deficit disorders (ADD) usually present themselves with symptoms of inattentiveness and disorganization, often accompanied by motor hyperactivity and impulsiveness (Beugin, 1990; Moghadam & Fagan, 1994). Teachers, parents, and other people who work with children should consult with a physician or psychologist before making an amateur diagnosis and putting children in a "box" from which it may be hard to escape. Some interventions designed to be of particular help for students with ADD may be helpful for all the children in a group or class.

> The teacher can provide a variety of cues, be understanding, and consult with other professionals when working with children who have various degrees of attention deficit disorder.

Once children begin to display ADD symptoms, they may encounter negative life experiences such as failure in school and getting into trouble with authority figures. These can lead the children into more "bad behavior," usually of a more serious nature, which in turn leads to more negative life experiences. This vicious cycle often continues into adult life. By the time the ADD symptoms have abated, the person is not in a good position to recoup on the lost positive life experiences. Many former attention deficit adults have turned to therapy and support groups in order to begin and continue leading productive lives. It is important that teachers respond quickly and in the child's best interest at the first sign of difficulty.

Teachers can help students struggling with ADD by providing strong cues and organizers. Some of these should be given before listening or reading to heighten motivation. During listening, the teacher can organize the information, highlight key points, and show the meaningfulness of the material. Post-listening strategies include verbal rehearsal and visualizing. These strategies will also help the students who do not have ADD. The activities recommended in this book have incorporated many of these suggestions or can be easily adapted to do so.

Mark, a nine-year-old student with whom Derek worked, displayed ADD symptoms. He was rarely on task. Sometimes he would kneel or crouch up with his feet on the chair and become preoccupied with what the other students were doing. He was not malicious or deliberately disobedient; in fact, Mark was eager to please, cheerful, and lively. Mark was not referred to a physician for diagnosis but might have benefited from such a referral.

ADD is a complex condition and our students deserve thoughtful care. For further expert information, please refer to the resources listed at the back of this book.

Social problems

A large number of statements in the list used for the survey of low achievement referred to difficulties in social behavior. About one-third of the students sampled were judged by their teachers to be badly behaved in class, to be immature in their relationships, to show off in front of other children, to find school irrelevant, to show little commitment or interest, and/or to experience social difficulties with their peers. It is interesting to note that the survey also showed that these kinds of problems were significantly more frequently associated with low-achieving boys than with low-achieving girls.

> Teachers can help students to stay on task by providing meaningful activities in a supportive environment.

Whether these factors are the cause of low achievement or its result is, of course, impossible to say. It seems likely that the frustration of constant failure in school generally (not just in mathematics) would contribute to antisocial behavior within the institution, just as much as a lack of social skills and unwillingness to cooperate with teachers and other students would contribute to the failure.

The frequent association of inappropriate social behavior with low achievement in mathematics appears to imply that teachers must aim to provide students with tasks to which they will commit themselves. It is not enough simply to demand that students undertake a task just because the teacher says so. The more we can provide our students with purposeful tasks which they themselves recognize as being worthwhile, the more likely we are to see some commitment and results.

Learned disability

Unfortunately, many students have been given subtle messages that they are not capable in mathematics. Graham (1994) reports that students gain information about the causes of their success or failure from messages given by teachers. These messages then become self-fulfilling prophesies. Often, well-intentioned teacher actions have negative effects on student motivation.

Researchers found that frequent criticism of the quality of one's work was positively related to high self-concept of ability in mathematics and high future expectations of success. Similarly, excessive praise for a student's failing effort gave the message that their ability was low. The absence of criticism was interpreted by students to mean that they had low ability. Holding high expectations for students, communicated through well-chosen criticism, expresses confidence and results in greater achievement.

Students seem to know that teachers are more likely to offer help to overcome uncontrollable factors like ability than controllable factors like effort. Supplying answers outright and offering help when there is no distress indicate that teachers have low estimates of student ability. Relative neglect communicates high expectations and assessment of ability. Instrumental help (probing when appropriate, answering questions, etc.) places more control with students and sends the message that they are capable.

Mathematics anxiety

About a quarter of the students sampled were judged by their teachers to show high levels of anxiety toward most tasks in school, and a similar proportion toward mathematics in particular. This is consistent with the previous comments about social behavior. Those students who are more accepting of the rules and conventions of the institution are likely to be more anxious about failing at the tasks set for them by the authorities within the institution. Since mathematics is the subject in which failure is experienced most overtly, a high level of anxiety toward the subject can be expected.

The challenge for the teacher is to foster self-confidence by providing experiences in learning mathematics which lead to success.

Again, it is not possible to determine whether this high degree of anxiety is a cause or an effect of low achievement in mathematics. This may be another case of one characteristic reinforcing the other. Repeated failure in mathematics intensifies the fear of further failure which then increases the level of anxiety; the high levels of anxiety inhibit the child's ability to learn and then his performance, and eventually lead to further failure.

Anxiety toward mathematics was a factor significantly more frequently associated with low-achieving girls than with low-achieving boys.

The failure/anxiety cycle could start from well-meaning peers trying to warn their unsuspecting friends about the deadly game of math! This anxiety would then create a condition that increases the chances of failure, providing yet another example of the self-fulfilling prophecy.

Two other students with whom Derek worked (eight-year-old Tracey and ten-year-old Sarah) both showed great "math anxiety." Tracey needed constant reassurance. She reverted to counting on her fingers even for small numbers when she encountered the least amount of difficulty. Sarah showed real panic and gave up the challenge quickly. Lack of persistence due to rising anxiety levels makes progress in mathematics unlikely and further math anxiety more likely.

The challenge for the teacher is to find ways of breaking this vicious circle, to reduce anxiety and thus foster the student's confidence in mathematics. One strategy is to use alternative testing methods. For students with high levels of anxiety toward mathematics, teaching strategies must lead to considerable experience of success. This will probably require that the teacher analyze the student's existing competence in mathematics and design a teaching program to build with very small steps.

Labels

We have chosen to call the subjects of this book "low achievers in mathematics" because this label does not imply any judgments about the reasons why the children concerned do not do as well in mathematics as might be hoped.

Less able children

Therefore, this book is not just about teaching mathematics to less able children. Although this might be an appropriate description of many students we have worked with over the years, we do not find the term "less able" a helpful one. It implies too strongly that the basis of the problem is the ability of the child. Once children are labeled in this way, the teacher's expectations of what they can achieve are inevitably limited. There are plenty of children in our schools who (compared to their peers) have low levels of achievement in mathematics who nevertheless have abilities which occasionally surface and surprise their teachers when they are given a task that motivates and excites them. The challenge for us as teachers, therefore, is to find ways of encouraging these abilities to emerge.

Slow learners

Nor is this a book about teaching mathematics to slow learners. This label seems to imply that all students follow the same learning path, but some proceed along it at a slower rate than others. Such a view of learning leads to the expectation that all students will work through exactly the same materials in mathematics lessons, with no allowance made for individual differences other than the rate of progress from one page of a commercially produced mathematics program to the next.

For example, low achievers may need considerably more practical work with coins and blocks, before moving on to recording a particular arithmetic operation with symbols, than might be provided by a program designed for average students (if there are any such "average" students in our classrooms). As well, some sections of the program could justifiably be omitted for some low achievers, at least temporarily. For example, we question the relative usefulness for many low achievers in this age group of tackling the section on volumes of cuboids which appears in most programs, or of learning to use exponential notation for representing squares, cubes, etc. The assumption, "It must be done because it is there," is clearly misguided. We cannot justify the view that our low-achieving students are simply slow learners and so they should just work through the same material as the others, but at their own rate.

Under-achievers

Another term which teachers often apply to students is under-achiever. This can be a helpful term if interpreted positively. If we call some children under-achievers, it might imply that we are optimistic that they have the potential, given the right encouragement and an appropriate curriculum, to achieve very much more than they are achieving at present. However, the term is often used in a negative sense, referring to students who achieve very little in school (often right across the curriculum) mainly because of their constant misbehavior, their antisocial attitudes, their inability to conform to institutional procedures, or their lack of interest in the tasks they are given in school.

Technically, the term under-achiever should apply to individuals whose achievement in a specific area is not commensurate with assessments of their general aptitude, such as a high score on an abilities test. It could apply to very bright individuals who could be leading the class but who are not. Our intention in this book is to provide support for teachers who work with students who are experiencing difficulty with mathematics, not merely performing below expectations.

Although many of the children who struggle with mathematics seem to struggle with most subjects in school, we do sometimes discover children who appear to have learning difficulties just in this specific area. In such cases, teachers understandably feel that there must be some reason why a child who otherwise does well at school is "under-achieving" in mathematics.

Low achievers

Other labels abound: special-needs, remedial, backward, dull, retarded, less gifted, and so on, each with its implied judgments about the nature or cause of the problem. By opting to focus on low achievment in mathematics, we are signaling what is essentially a descriptive, pragmatic approach. There are many children who in fact achieve very much less in this subject than most other children of their age. The reasons for this are varied, complex, somewhat idiosyncratic, and often unpredictable, but nevertheless, based on our experience of working with such children and their teachers, it is clear to us that there is much we can do to help them make progress and grow in confidence. Many children will move out of the grouping we call low achievers in mathematics as a result of the help that we provide.

So this book is concerned with teaching mathematics to all kinds of low-achieving children in the eight- to twelve-year age range: children who just do not do very well at the subject, whether less able, slow learning, under-achieving, or whatever else they might be labeled. These children find themselves permanently in the bottom class for mathematics in those schools that use ability groupings; or they are always one or two books behind the majority of the class in those schools where children work individually through a series of workbooks in a mathematics program; or they are in what the teacher identifies as the remedial group within a mixed ability class, the children who need special help and programming in mathematics. Typically these children would be able to get very few questions correct if they were given a norm-referenced assessment test in mathematics, and would have standardized scores which put them in the bottom 25% of a national ability range for their peer group. This book was written for these children.

 # QUESTIONS FOR DISCUSSION WITH COLLEAGUES

1. Which characteristics are exhibited by the low achievers you know?
2. Is it important to know what may be causing the difficulties in mathematics experienced by our students? What would you do as a result of having that information?
3. What labels are used by teachers in your work setting to describe students who appear to need extra help with mathematics? How helpful are these descriptors?

2 Important Considerations in Teaching Mathematics

Four fundamental considerations in teaching mathematics

If we are ever going to hear exclamations of joy from students who are thinking about or working with mathematics, we need to teach in a way that is rewarding and interesting. In this section we outline our basic approach to the teaching of mathematics, which can help all students as well as low achievers.

Synthesizing the National Council of Teachers of Mathematics (NCTM) *Professional Standards for Teaching Mathematics* (1991) and other guidelines for effective practice, we have organized important considerations for teaching mathematics into the following four categories:

1. The particular **tasks** given to students shape their opportunities for learning.
2. A rich learning **environment** in the classroom allows students to construct for themselves the meaning of mathematics and encourages growth in mathematical power and literacy.
3. The **resources** and tools made available to students enhance learning opportunities.

4. **Teachers** contribute to the improvement of the teaching/learning process by analyzing and reflecting on their own teaching and the learning of their students.

1. Tasks that make students think

According to the NCTM *Professional Standards for Teaching Mathematics* (p. 25), a task is the stimulus for student thinking about concepts, procedures, connections, and applications and provides a context for skill development. Tasks should
- require that students reason mathematically;
- encourage the development of conceptual understandings;
- stimulate connections and communication;
- involve problem setting, problem solving, and mathematical reasoning;
- be stimulating and motivating;
- utilize and be sensitive toward diverse student backgrounds and experiences and
- engage students in what mathematicians actually do.

Students learn mathematics by doing mathematics.

The Western Canadian Protocol (1996) places great emphasis on activities which involve doing mathematics: "At all levels, students benefit from working with appropriate materials, tools, and contexts when constructing personal meaning about new mathematical ideas" (p. 2).

Problem situations are superb tasks for building mathematical reasoning and skills. The NCTM (1991, p. 26) recommended that problem solving be embedded throughout the instruction of mathematics. Teachers should
- find problems that match the intended content, are motivating, and address student learning needs and
- provide frequent opportunities to pose and solve good quality problems.

Problem solving requires understanding the problem, choosing an approach, trying it out, and justifying a solution to others. To be successful, students need generic skills such as reading, computing, estimating, and mental calculation.

In working with low achievers, our most important targets must be in the area of numeracy.

Our experience of working with students who do not do well at mathematics has convinced us that much of the problem is that they are overloaded with the "basics" of computation: routine tasks which have no meaning or purpose for them whatsoever. Tasks built around narrow learning targets of knowledge, techniques, and skills provide students, including low achievers, with no satisfaction or incentive for learning (particularly if their most frequent experience is of getting the answers wrong). One of the major motives for this book is to promote mathematical understanding in our students. Much of the satisfaction inherent in learning mathematics lies in understanding our mathematical environment by making connections, relating the symbols of mathematics to real-life situations, seeing how things fit together, and articulating the patterns and relationships which are fundamental to our number system and number operations. This can best be done with purposeful tasks in meaningful contexts which make students think.

In our view, a numerate person is one who can cope confidently with the numerical situations they encounter in normal everyday life. An innumerate person is likely to be so lacking in this confidence that they unquestioningly accept the opinions and judgments of others when numbers and numerical interpretation are involved. Knowing what to enter on a calculator in an everyday numerical situation is an example of what we would regard as a basic component of numeracy.

A numerate person has at least some idea of the size of answer expected and its meaning to the issue under consideration, and is thus less at the mercy of the unscrupulous or misguided. To this end, estimation skills must be considered as an integral part of any program in numeracy. Estimates and approximations are used often in real-life situations and need to be thoroughly understood.

Estimates can increase clarity and help focus on the essential concepts and ideas by removing distracting and unnecessary details. When estimating, students need to think through what they are doing and why, rather than just perform a procedure or use an algorithm. Estimation procedures can lead to new insights about exact procedures and can be used to check the work done on calculators with exact numbers. One of the most important outcomes of estimating is that students are encouraged to think about their mathematical thinking, an essential activity for developing solid understandings (Cardelle-Elawar, 1992).

In Chapter 6 we discuss how students can use a calculator to solve everyday problems. These efforts need to be supported by estimation skills so that students have a clear idea of what they are doing and have some confidence in the result obtained from the calculator.

In this book we have excluded spatial relationships, other than the concepts associated with measurement, but we are not suggesting that this topic should have no part in the mathematical development of low achievers. Some who struggle with numerical work can have both their confidence and their motivation boosted through success with spatial tasks, and many of them gain particular satisfaction from exploring geometric patterns. We have chosen to concentrate on those topics which usually present particular challenges to teachers of low achievers and which are seen as top priorities. Other reputable texts and teacher resource books are helpful in teaching spatial skills.

It is also important to focus specifically on language development in teaching mathematics to low-achieving students. As we saw in the last chapter, poor language skills (reading, writing, listening, and even speaking) are often associated with low achievement in mathematics. Mathematics has its own peculiar language patterns and vocabulary, and a major part of the development of understanding of mathematics must focus on building up confidence in handling these and in connecting them with the corresponding mathematical symbols and manipulation of concrete materials. Rather than addressing these using a drill-and-practice approach, we recommend challenging students in purposeful and meaningful contexts which we explain in detail later in this chapter.

> The activities found in other chapters provide excellent opportunities for students to verbalize their understandings and to make connections among words, symbols, and mathematical concepts.

2. Environments that encourage students to think

"If we want students to learn to make conjectures, experiment with alternative approaches to solving problems, and construct and respond to others' mathematical arguments, then creating an environment that fosters these kinds of activities is essential" (NCTM, 1991, p. 56.)

One element of a rich environment is social interaction (Jennings & Di, 1996; Day et al. 1985). Teachers have the responsibility to initiate and maintain a rich cooperative learning environment in which students are encouraged to:

It is the teacher's responsibility to create and maintain an environment which promotes student thinking.

- reason mathematically (justifying, verifying, revising, and discarding claims based on convincing arguments) with the teacher and peers;
- ask questions and acknowledge confusion openly (again, with the teacher and peers);
- take one another seriously; and
- accept some responsibility for helping one another.

The teacher encourages students to reason by carefully selecting tasks and using probing questions, by listening more, by providing information and leading students, and by monitoring student participation in groups and pairs. One effective way of learning mathematics is to talk and write about new understandings, relationships, and insights (Davison & Pearce, 1988; Miller, 1991). Writing in particular causes learners to pause and reflect on those connections that consolidate the learning. Writing also practices the use of mathematical language and symbols. It can be done in conjunction with conversations with other students, either before or after talking about the lesson. Often, low achievers are embarrassed to ask questions but they will write, given support and encouragement. And reading the students' writing about math will provide teachers with insights into what and how students are learning.

Cooperative learning can make a strong contribution toward creating an enriched environment, but it is more than just putting students into groups. It is learning and working together toward a common goal. Successful cooperative learning is based on the presence of five elements.

1. *Group interaction:* Students benefit from working with groups of classmates, made up of students with a mix of ability and other characteristics. Groups can be formed by the teacher or the students, or through a random process. When first trying cooperative learning in small groups, teachers may want to begin with pairs and then increase the size of the groups to four or five. A group of three is also a practical, effective size.

2. *Use and development of social skills:* Like problem-solving skills, these skills can be taught, practiced, and extended. Brainstorming sessions, role plays, discussions, and simulations can be used to identify, teach, and reinforce social skills such as listening attentively and respectfully, using a soft voice, staying on task, returning materials, asking questions, and challenging thoughts, not persons.

3. *Positive interdependence among group members:* Common goals, rewards, and resources, along with complementary and interconnected roles, encourage and require sharing among group members. Sample roles include the following:
   - the facilitator promotes participation and task completion,
   - the recorder presents the group responses or solutions,
   - the time-keeper watches the time taken for each of the sub-tasks to keep the group from unproductive work,
   - the encourager could be a role all agree to accept, and

- the materials manager handles the resources or other equipment needed by the group.

4. *Individual accountability:* Each member of the group must be held accountable for the learning and contributions of each other as well as themselves. If all students understand and agree how they will be individually accountable before they become involved in the cooperative group activity, they are more likely to respond positively. Here are some suggestions (each with its own advantages and disadvantages):
   - select one or two members of each group to take a short quiz,
   - pick one or two members from each group to present the group product to the class,
   - require all student signatures on the assignments,
   - rotate the different roles among group members, and
   - ensure that the task cannot be completed by students working independently (like a group report) but requires agreement and consensus (such as solving a problem or arriving at a decision).

5. *Reflection:* Thinking and communicating about the cooperative learning experiences will likely lead to greater awareness of the learning process, improved group and individual performance, and greater reliance on intrinsic rewards. The use of journals and group de-briefing sessions can promote useful reflection about the group process and one's role in it.

> In this book are many ideas for games and small group activities to help provide the environment which allows students to think. Teachers are encouraged to adapt them as required.

There continues to be some controversy regarding homogeneous ability groupings of students (Peterson, 1989). Studies generally indicate that putting low achieving students together in the same room does not help them as much as having them work in mixed ability classroom settings. Our view is that the best interests of the students must be kept foremost. A rich environment that encourages students to think is our goal and this can be achieved in both mixed and homogeneous groupings of students.

3. Resources that help students think

Resources and technology of all kinds can encourage student mathematical reasoning. Calculators, computers, concrete materials, pictorial representations, terms and symbols, and metaphors (as well as written and spoken language) can all help students to express and think about mathematical ideas at higher levels. Such resources should be used when they provide access to richer mathematics, permit greater learning, and allow students to grapple with more interesting and realistic problems rather than simply entertaining, amusing, or otherwise occupying students. Therefore, devote time to free exploration, distribution, and collection routines, and inform parents and other staff of the purposes of the resources.

Calculators

Studies have shown that the use of calculators can improve computational skills slightly and problem-solving skills moderately (Neilsen, 1995; NCTM, 1992). With calculators, students experience increased motivation, self-confidence, persistence, and a greater willingness to delve into problems more deeply. Since calculators increase the accuracy of and reduce the time taken for lengthy, tedious computations, all students are free to become more engaged in the thinking demanded by problem solving, reasoning, exploration of patterns, communication, and application of knowledge to new situations. Estimation and mental computation skills become more important as a check on the reasonableness of solutions obtained with a calculator.

Students who use calculators should be trained to be discriminating and to use them when appropriate to do so. It is not advisable to use calculators when introducing a new concept; unfamiliar ideas should first be learned in meaningful contexts with concrete materials or representations.

Computers

Computers are well suited to helping students focus more on the thinking required to do mathematics than on the mechanics of producing graphs, doing multiple computations, and finding and manipulating data. Computer software (including spreadsheets and data bases) is available which provides an interactive focus on various kinds of problem formulating and solving. Teachers interested in moving into or expanding their computer use in the classroom for instruction would find Heide and Henderson's (1994) book very helpful.

Throughout the book we have suggested relevant materials which will help students to develop a solid understanding of the concepts.

Manipulatives

Manipulatives help students to construct justifiable understandings of mathematics for themselves (indeed, no one can do it for them!) and to illustrate and communicate their reasoning. Concrete materials encourage active participation in consolidating and exploring mathematical ideas. They are a means to deeper mathematical understanding.

4. Teachers who want students to think

"To improve their mathematics instructions teachers must constantly analyze what they and their students are doing and how that is affecting what the students are learning" (NCTM, 1991, p. 67). Teaching mathematics is a complex social activity. It is not reducible to recipes; it is influenced by sophisticated norms which are socially constructed and enacted. To change mathematics instruction for the better, teachers need to gather accurate information about student learning and mathematics, reflect on the data individually and collectively, and collaborate with other teachers to find better ways to help students learn successfully. Any teacher wanting to change the way mathematics is taught in his or her school will need to work with other teachers over the long term. Hopefully this book will prove to be a key resource.

To promote teacher collegiality we have included questions for discussion at the end of each chapter.

Constructivism

Many educators and parents have heard of the term "constructivism," read about it, or studied it in university classes. Since much of what we have espoused in this book finds a theoretical home in this theory of learning, we will provide a brief explanation. Although there is great debate over definitions and foundations of the theory itself (Cobb, 1994; Phillips, 1995), we point out some of the key elements. Basically, constructivism says that the process of thinking builds up connections (Haylock & Cockburn, 1997) which we interpret as understanding (APA, 1993). When children encounter some new experience, they understand it if they can connect it to previous experiences or, better yet, to a network of previously connected experiences. With appropriate guidance, students can be helped to learn not only well-structured skills but higher level thinking strategies (Rosenshine & Meister, 1992; Gallimore & Tharp, 1990). They demonstrate their new understanding by showing that they can use or express what they have learned in different contexts. The more strongly connected the experience, the more we say that they understand it.

Learning without making connections is what we would regard as learning by rote. Such learning is easily confused or forgotten, particularly by many low achievers with poor memories, and is of little value in application to real-life situations.

Figure 2.1 illustrates one of the systems of connections that students need to make when learning mathematical concepts. Students need to relate what they hear about the world with the symbols that mathematics uses to express ideas and with pictures of concepts and concrete (real) situations. For example, the addition of two numbers is encountered in everyday life when we shop. The language we use to express the situation of having two items and wanting to know how much we need to pay in total must be related to the act of collecting them together, the mathematical symbols used to show addition, and pictorial representations of the collected items. In Chapter 6 we elaborate on classes of addition problems, but for now we simply point out that children have many important connections to make in order to learn mathematics.

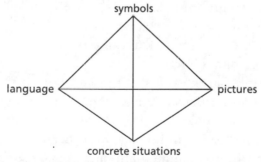

FIGURE 2.1 *Necessary connections to succeed at mathematics.*

Purposeful activities in meaningful contexts

Our experience suggests that when we find purposeful, meaningful tasks, students can show unexpected competence and determination to succeed. Furthermore, learning in the context for which the skill is intended enables students to transfer their learning to other similar problems (Cognition and Technology Group, 1992).

> Situations in realistic contexts are opportunities to apply mathematics and, conversely, the mathematics learned is used to solve problems in practical situations (Meyer, 1997).

Two Illustrations

An impressive illustration of this assertion is provided by the following problem:

"How much will it cost to purchase enough orange juice to provide three drinks each for 90 participants in a soccer tournament if a large jug of concentrated orange juice costs $2.15 and can be diluted at a ratio of 2 parts water to 1 part juice."

A group of eight- and nine year-olds, in what was called a low-ability grouping for mathematics, found themselves having to solve this problem when they were given responsibility for providing refreshments for an inter-school soccer tournament (Haylock et al., 1985). Of course, it was not presented to them in this form. Their task was to organize the drinks, so they had to find out how many bottles of concentrated juice to buy and set a budget. Gradually they determined what information would be needed to solve the problem. They found out from other groups planning related aspects of the event that three drinks per person would be required during the day and that there were 90 participants. They found out the price of juice from the local supermarket. They then did some direct measurement to determine how many cups could be poured from one jug, and how many jugs would be needed in total. One boy gained a significant insight from this activity, shown by the remark he made to his teacher while working on the problem: "You can use adding for this, Miss. I reckon this is why we learn it, so we can use it (addition) for things."

They then realized that the bottled juice had to be diluted and decided to do some market research (using children in their class and trial and error) to determine the ratio of water to juice. Using their own informal methods, which made sense to them in that context, and, incidentally, without using a calculator, they decided they needed to buy four jugs of concentrated juice and put in a budget of $8.60. In the process, they amazed their teacher by both their commitment to the task and their success with the mathematics involved.

> Time and time again low-achieving students surprise their teachers with what they can do when they are given purposeful tasks, real problems, and the opportunity to use mathematics to make things happen.

On another occasion Derek worked with a teacher and a group of low-achieving 10- and 11-year-olds, and found the students making very little headway with some exercises in their mathematics workbooks. The books presented the students with some drawings of play money ($10, $20, $50, and $100), and the instructions said to shade the bills required to make up various amounts. This is a typical example of the purposeless activities that students are often asked to undertake in mathematics lessons. Given the students' sense of frustration, they abandoned these exercises (in fact, the school abandoned the program!). Instead, the children were put into groups of four, given a supply of play money, and challenged to find as many different ways of making up $190 as they could, recording their answers in the form of a table. The actual mathematical skills being developed were exactly the same as those in the exercises they had abandoned, but the difference in the students' perfor-

> Students can make much more progress with greater speed when given tasks with meaning and purpose that make them think.

mance was quite dramatic. They were engaged in a task with some purpose and connection to their real world and which allowed them to work with their peers. Most of the groups found about 30 solutions to the problem, with one group coming up with all 34 possibilities. This was quite an achievement for students who were supposed to be poor at mathematics, and who had, in the previous lesson, failed at a corresponding (but purposeless) task in their mathematics book.

Through these projects students were engaged in authentic problem solving. They were learning life skills and mathematics at the same time. This is what Hope (1993) means when he talks about teaching *via* problems, as opposed to teaching *about* problems or *for* problem-solving.

Relevance

There seems to be general agreement that mathematics, particularly for low-achieving students, must be made more relevant. It is of the utmost importance that the mathematical work of children in remedial classes should not consist of the practice of arithmetical skills in isolation, but should be accompanied by discussion of the concepts on which these skills rest and the ways in which they can be used in the children's everyday lives.

Many teachers and other educators have differing ideas of what is meant by "relevance." We suggest four ways in which this notion is used in mathematics teaching.

1. *Vicarious relevance*

    The following mathematical problems might appear to be relevant to students:
    - Look at the bus schedules for Los Angeles to San Francisco and San Francisco to Portland; what time should I catch a bus from Los Angeles to get to Portland by 6:00 pm?
    - My living room is 4 m by 6 m; what will it cost me to carpet it if the carpet costs $6.75 per square metre?

    These are real problems, but they are not the student's problems. The student is neither traveling nor laying carpet in her living room. She is being asked to solve someone else's problem. This is what we term "vicarious relevance." Mathematics textbooks are filled with questions of this kind, asking the student to solve a problem on behalf of someone else, and we cannot imagine that any mathematics teacher could manage without recourse to them. The mathematics is at least embedded in a meaningful context. But often this type of problem fails to motivate students to commit themselves to its solution, because the activity lacks any real purpose for them.

2. *Artificial relevance*

    In a second way of making mathematics relevant, called "artificial relevance," the teacher makes use of situations or contexts which are of interest to the students as a basis for generating some mathematical activity. This approach, drawing on students' interests in such things as sport, television schedules, and pop music charts, can be effective. For example, with one group of nine- and ten-year-olds, Derek took the idea of "goal difference" to rank soccer teams with the same number of points as an introduction to negative numbers. The students were motivated by their interest in soccer to engage in the mathematical activity. The context gave meaning to the mathematical ideas, but once again the problems posed were, to be honest, artificial and lacking in any real purpose. For these kinds of problems the mathematics is related to real life, is interesting, but is not being used to do anything purposeful.

Teachers can sometimes make use of artificial relevance by incorporating mathematical activity into other school subjects. Often teachers miss the opportunity to do this, keeping mathematics as an isolated experience unrelated to anything else children do in school. For example, a group doing an integrated project on transportation might collect data about the different ways in which students travel to school, organize these data, display them in graphical form, and interpret the results. The mathematics is thus relevant, in the sense that it is related to other activities in which the student is engaged, but it lacks genuine purpose.

> Teachers can refer to the 1995 NCTM Yearbook for many excellent suggestions on how to effectively accomplish integration across subjects.

3. *"Some-time-in-the-future" relevance*

A feeble approach to making mathematics relevant is to try to persuade our reluctant learners that the mathematical skills we are trying to teach them will be useful for them when they leave school or are in the next grade. Often this is no more than an admission by the teachers that they do not actually know themselves what is the point of the students learning the material in question. On the whole, an appeal to long-term relevance is unsuccessful in motivating students. However, Derek recalled an occasion when experienced workmen were doing major renovations in the school at the same time as the students were learning about length measurement. The situation seemed to imbue the students' own practical work with some degree of relevance. He was able to draw their attention to the way the same measurement skills were being used all around them by the workmen.

4. *Immediate and genuine relevance*

Undoubtedly, we should be aiming for immediate and genuine relevance — where students are using mathematics to achieve something which matters to them at the time, as in the illustration of juice for the soccer tournament. There is a considerable body of evidence that students will achieve much more and show greater commitment when they are engaged in tasks with immediate and genuine relevance.

Even children as young as nine years, who, for some reason happen to be involved in everyday commercial transactions, seem to be able to construct quite complex mathematical strategies for solving problems and can achieve success where they would fail at the identical mathematical task presented as either a word problem or as a context-free computation (Carraher et al., 1985, 1988).

> The challenge for teachers is to try to find ways of giving mathematics in school a degree of immediate and genuine relevance: Using mathematics to make things happen.

When students are committed to a task in which they have to use mathematics to make something that matters to them happen, then mathematics becomes immediately and genuinely relevant. Some students investigated a shower unit at school. They produced such a convincing case that the parents' group donated a large sum of money toward the cost of their recommendations. The students had made something happen.

Often, these students are spatially oriented, want to manipulate real objects, and are interested in technology. The reference book, *All Aboard: Cross-Curricular Design and Technology Strategies and Activities* (1996), edited by Julie Czerneda, provides excellent suggestions for using ready-made and teacher-developed technology activities for our students. These easy-to-use ideas are likely to help you find or design meaningful and purposeful projects for students in the technology area.

Categories of purposeful activities

Students find a wide range of activities purposeful, and a number of categories might be suggested. These are not hard and fast categories, and they are not suggested as a method of analyzing or classifying activities. Rather, they are proposed as a framework for generating ideas for useful learning experiences for low-achieving students in mathematics. These categories are solving a real problem, planning an event, designing and constructing, engaging in a simulation or role play, games, and competition. Figure 2.2 shows the categories of purposeful activities together with types of meaningful contexts to create a useful chart.

While games and competitions are purposeful activities, they provide their own meaningful context and criteria for success. Consequently, we have not included separate cells in Figure 2.2 under games and competitions.

MEANINGFUL CONTEXTS	PURPOSEFUL ACTIVITIES				
	solving a real problem	planning an event	design and construction	simulation/ role play	games and competition
School Organization					
Classroom					
TV and Video					
Life at Home					
Shopping					
Fund-raising					
Cooking					
Travel					
Sport					
Other					

FIGURE 2.2 *Purposeful activities and meaningful contexts*

Real problems in the context of the school organization might include setting up a staff and visitor parking area at school or deciding how to spend money allocated to sports equipment. Planning an event could include setting up a juice stand for a sports tournament as previously described. A desing and construction task could be to make a box or storage shelf for classroom materials. Within the constraints of our school organization we may not be able to allow students to develop their mathematical skills through planning actual events, through solving real problems, or by undertaking the design and construction of something useful, as often as we might wish. However, we may find that students show persistence and motivation in simulations of real-life problems or activities. A range of very effective computer software of this kind is now available. Computer simulations may even allow students the opportunity to make decisions about the values of the variables which determine the degree of success or failure of their endeavors.

Role play is an activity that works with some students. They can act out a real situation, such as a family dispute over an allowance, and then seek to solve the problems which emerge.

Finally most children enjoy participating in games and competitions. These categories of activities have some purpose from the student's perspective, namely, to be the winner or to enjoy the socialization or challenge. We can harness students' willingness to commit themselves to playing a game, or to participating in a competition, in order to develop their mathematical skills. Games and competitions are often used much more specifically to target particular objectives than the other purposeful activities suggested above.

A disadvantage of competitive games is that they may isolate certain students who do not do well. An overuse of games which emphasize winning and losing also encourages a particular motivational orientation in students which may eventually lead to less persistence and effort (Ames & Ames, 1984) and may also undermine the cooperative spirit of the students.

Meaningful contexts

Alongside the categories of purposeful activities, we suggest several categories of meaningful contexts. By "meaningful context" we mean some aspect of the student's everyday experience in which mathematics is or can be embedded. Two examples of such meaningful contexts are the school organization and the classroom. You may want to add to our list of meaningful contexts. In these two contexts, students encounter problems they can make sense of and in which they are actively involved. Solving the problem of where the staff should park their cars, or deciding on the best arrangement of the furniture in the classroom, or planning the school dance, or dealing with the class monthly book club order, for example, are all tasks which have real purpose and which arise in contexts which students understand. They know what the task is about, they can recognize a solution when it is achieved, and they appreciate the criteria which are significant in the context concerned. These are meaningful contexts for the development and application of their mathematical knowledge, skills, and understanding.

Each cell in Figure 2.2 might suggest various purposeful activities in meaningful contexts which would allow the development and application of the students' mathematics skills. For example, the intersection of "travel" and "planning an event" suggests that a group of students could be given responsibility for planning the travel arrangements for a class trip. This is something which teachers might normally do themselves, thus missing the opportunity to give their students a purposeful task in a meaningful context, with considerable potential for developing and using mathematical knowledge. The intersection of "cooking" and "designing and constructing" might remind teachers of the mathematics involved in baking a cake. "Solving a real problem" and "fund-raising" might lead us to give our students responsibility for handling a charity drive.

Some of the computer programs available which simulate the running of small businesses include a tuck shop, a stall at a school fair, and a car wash. These would come in the category of "engaging in a simulation" set in the meaningful context of "earning money." Students make decisions about the purchase of materials, the prices they will charge, and how much they will spend on advertising, all of which affect their earnings in an imaginary business. Simple simulations such as these call upon and develop a wide range of relevant mathematical skills and are often very effective as purposeful activities for many students.

Key teaching points

- Tasks should be chosen to ensure that students need to reason mathematically
- Rich intellectual environments are best; cooperative learning strategies have many advantages
- A variety of resources should be made available to students for appropriate use, including calculators and computers
- Teachers should regularly reflect on their practice of teaching mathematics in order to continue improving
- Use purposeful activities in meaningful contexts

 QUESTIONS FOR DISCUSSION WITH COLLEAGUES

1. In what ways has our framework for looking at mathematics instruction (tasks, environments, resources, and teachers) been helpful to you?
2. What do you understand by "purposeful activities in meaningful contexts"? Is this a realistic and worthwhile approach in teaching mathematics to your students?
3. Evaluate a recent mathematics lesson you taught or observed. From the perspective of the students, how "purposeful" were the tasks in which they were engaged? Can you give some examples from your own teaching experiences where you involved students in purposeful activities in meaningful contexts?
4. What special challenges do you face in trying to teach your students mathematics, especially in trying to help low achievers learn?

3 Why Mathematics Is So Hard to Learn

FEATURES OF THIS CHAPTER

- some characteristics of the way mathematics is sometimes taught that make it a difficult subject to learn, especially for low achieving students

- ways we can improve our teaching of mathematics to help students succeed

Characteristics of school mathematics and the way it is taught

Mathematics is a distinctive subject with its own particular ways of proceeding and its own characteristic concepts and ways of manipulating and relating these concepts together. Students need to learn mathematics not just to attain high-tech jobs, but to understand the world around us and to feel the sense of personal satisfaction when things make sense (Sutton, 1997). Unfortunately, "today's math class consists of eight years of paper-and-pencil computations in arithmetic — done the way it was done back when my mother was in school and for more than 300 years before that — drill and rote with no end in sight" (Neilsen, 1995). It may be helpful for those who teach children with particular difficulties in mathematics to be explicitly aware of some of the characteristics of the subject which may contribute to learning difficulties and then to reflect on what we, as teachers, can do about them. To be more effective, we need to change the way math is generally taught in schools.

Right or wrong

It has always seemed to us to be particularly significant that in mathematics, more than in any other aspect of the school curriculum, students are given tasks for which their responses will be judged absolutely right or absolutely wrong. This characteristic of mathematics gives many students so much motivation: they get things absolutely right, ten out of ten, checkmarks abound. They experience frequent success and this is, for them, a very satisfying experience. But for those students at the other end of the spectrum, constant failure, repeated judgment that their responses are wrong, and red x's populating their exercise books all add up to a depressing and frustrating experience. Negative comments in their other activities in school are rarely so final. Their creative writing might be judged to be "rather flat"; their descriptive writing might provoke the comment, "you have missed out some important points"; they might be told that their drawings are "scruffy," their attempts at scientific observation and recording "careless"; and so on. In mathematics, more than in any other subject, they can experience absolute failure at the tasks they are given.

"Many, if not most, students come to perceive math as a system of techniques that someone wise has invented, which they need to memorize in order to get the right answers on a series of problems that are not particularly interesting to them so they can graduate and stop studying mathematics." (Weissglass, 1984, p. 295.)

When teachers and students think that doing math is simply finding the right answers, students are taught to follow certain algorithms (formal routines for dealing with calculations such as addition or subtraction) to obtain the correct solutions to exercises, a task for which calculators are often better suited. Many students find it difficult to remember and make sense of all the steps of the algorithms and, in their genuine attempts to get the right answer, they fail miserably (only to be told that they need to try harder!). But often, many students are capable of developing and using their own informal, unconventional, ways of dealing with calculations. These are necessarily based on the student's own understanding of the mathematical structure of the problem and the relationships between the numbers involved. Informal methods represent student thinking and focus on the process of mathematics. Using and justifying informal methods is another way of having students think about their own mathematical thinking. This is important for the growth of deep understanding (Cardelle-Elawar, 1992).

Another consequence of seeing and teaching mathematics as a science of precision is the tendency to focus on those tasks which have clear and correct answers and to think that this is mathematics. Such a focus relies heavily on disembodied tasks and purpose-less activities. There is considerable evidence that students are much more capable of learning and demonstrating mathematical skills when tasks are embedded in a context that makes sense to them (Donaldson, 1978, Hughes, 1986). An intriguing study of Brazilian children (Saxe, 1988), for example, found that many 10- to 12-year-olds with minimal schooling, who worked as street candy-sellers, had developed a level of performance for handling money and ratios using complex, but informal, mathematical skills that was far superior to that of children who attended school regularly. Teachers need to teach skills that have real life connections and do not necessarily yield precise, absolute answers.

Cumulative effect of failure

One other subject in schools which shares this feature of absolute judgments of right or wrong is spelling. But there is a significant difference here. If we cannot spell a particular word, this does not usually stop us from trying to learn to spell other words, nor does it prevent us from using the word we cannot spell correctly in talking, reading, or even in writing across the curriculum. But if students cannot succeed with a particular mathematical skill, they may find it almost impossible to succeed with a whole host of related mathematical skills because of the hierarchical nature of much of mathematics.

Failure to master one area of mathematics may make it impossible to move ahead into other areas with a high degree of success.

For example, if a student cannot master addition of numbers up to 10, he would probably not succeed in subtraction with these numbers, with addition of two-digit numbers, and so on. Furthermore, he may also fail at many practical, problem-solving tasks, such as shopping and handling money, because of a lack of knowledge of addition. This cumulative effect of failure is a more distinctive characteristic of learning mathematics than of most other aspects of school learning.

Often, when being taught mathematics, a child may be moved on to the next process to be learned before the previous one is thoroughly mastered and understood. The result of this shortcoming is often total confusion in the child's mind, particularly when the processes are taught by rote. It is quite distressing at times to see children struggling with a routine such as subtraction of three-digit numbers by borrowing, crossing out zeros, writing little ones and nines apparently at random, and confusing the addition process with the subtraction. Here a child has been pushed ahead when there is little understanding of the operations, when the concrete meaning of the abstractions has been lost, and when the only connection with the child's experiences is several layers removed. Spending adequate time with students who are working through certain ideas and relationships may seem a slow way to proceed, but it will pay dividends of time and confidence in later areas of study. Teachers need to resist the temptation to speed up in order to cover all the curriculum requirements if it means that the students will remain confused and frustrated.

Accuracy and concentration

Success in school mathematics often requires a considerable degree of care and accuracy. Students need to concentrate on their tasks and be self-disciplined in their approach to their work in mathematics, often in a way that is alien to students in our contemporary western society. Growing up in a world dominated by fast-moving television, videos, instant entertainment, and popular culture, many young people are conditioned to lose interest in anything that requires concentration for more than two minutes. Consequently, some aspects of learning mathematics successfully may require some personal and social development in the areas of patience, care, accuracy, concentration, and self-discipline, which, for some students, will be a considerable undertaking.

> To be successful in mathematics, children need to use concentration and care — work habits that many have not yet acquired.

Lack of concentration on the task at hand is a common characteristic of children with attention deficit disorder (ADD) (see Chapter 1). They appear unable to refrain from reacting to any external stimulus, such as movement of other children around the room, conversations, activity seen through the windows, and so on. Since mathematical tasks require concentration, it is not surprising that these children make little progress with this subject.

Teaching routines and recipes for manipulating symbols without any basis in understanding is sure to rob children of the inherent motivation derived from understanding relationships in mathematics and learning to comprehend the world around them. Poor concentration and carelessness may be intensified by a lack of motivation. Teachers, parents, and other educators must help students to form secure connections between their manipulations of real world things (such as money and blocks), the language they use to describe these manipulations, and the symbols they use to record and communicate them (see Figure 2.1). They also need to appeal to students' natural curiosity and sense of wonderment. If students understand that their efforts result in a real payoff, making them more able to make sense of the world around them, they are more likely to face the challenge of concentrating.

Many teaching techniques that work well for children with ADD can enhance the teaching/learning experience for all students. In one method, teachers use multiple channels in communicating with students, such as reinforcing the visual, tactile, or memory cues given in some exercises with auditory cues (Bley & Thornton, 1981).

Abstractions and Symbols

> Learning is complicated because mathematics is a science of short cuts. Mathematical reality is "simplified" into abstract concepts represented by symbols.

A major difficulty for many students is that mathematics inherently deals so much with abstract concepts. From the earliest years of schooling, the symbols and language of mathematics are used to represent abstractions and the relationships between abstractions. The symbol "5," for example, might represent the attribute shared by all concrete examples of sets of five things. When it is used on its own, unattached to a specific set, it is an abstraction. A simple mathematical statement such as "3 + 5 = 8" is then a relationship between the abstractions 3, 5, and 8. The whole statement is an abstraction derived from all the examples experienced of putting together sets of 3 things and 5 things and finding you have a set of 8 things. Of course, the abstractions represented by mathematical symbols (at least at this level) can always be traced back to concrete experiences with real things, but this gets more and more difficult as new mathematical concepts are developed by a process of abstracting from abstractions. For example, "multiples of 3" is a concept formed by an abstraction of the attribute shared by the abstractions 3, 6, 9, 12, and so on, and is therefore two steps removed from the concrete experiences of manipulating sets of counters, fingers, or other objects.

An important aspect of school mathematics is the application of numerical and spatial concepts and skills to various kinds of measurement. This gives students much opportunity for direct, practical application of mathematical ideas. However, many concepts of measuring things such as volume, mass, and time are themselves very abstract and require a highly sophisticated degree of organization of one's perceptions in order to focus on the particular attribute being measured. Many students who find mathematics difficult show a range of immature misunderstandings and confusions about such fundamental, but abstract, concepts of measurement. Derek observed a ten-year-old boy comparing the capacity of two containers by filling one with water and pouring it into the other. The boy then insisted that the smaller one was the bigger because the larger one was only half-full, whereas the smaller one had been full right to the top.

> The symbols used in mathematics add to its power and its "short cuts" but also make it more formidable to learn.

Mathematics is also complex because of its characteristic use of symbols to represent and to manipulate abstract concepts. However, the use of symbols gives power to mathematics. As these manipulations get further and further away from the real contexts which give them meaning and purpose, the subject becomes more and more bewildering for many students.

But there is a further, peculiar difficulty in the way symbols are used in mathematics, particularly in the area of number and number operations. This is the potentially confusing practice of using one symbol to represent more than one category of experience. For example, the division symbol in "18 ÷ 6" could mean in concrete terms "share a set of 18 counters equally among 6 people and see how many they each get." But it could also mean: "put a set of 18 counters into groups of 6 and see how many groups there are." The same symbol "÷" is used here in two very different ways, both valid models for the mathematical concept of "division." This is not an isolated example, since similar things occur with the symbols and concepts of addition, subtraction, multiplication, fractions, and even the symbols for numbers themselves. For example, Figure 3.1 shows just some of the great variety of concrete experiences which a young child may have to learn to connect with the symbol "5" and the word "five": a set of five counters, a line of five counters and then a longer line with the same number, a familiar pattern for five shown in the dots on a domino, a point labeled "5" on a number line, a square labeled "5" on a board game, five years of age, five cubes joined together, a room or a house labeled number five, a 5¢ coin, and a set of three coins worth $5. Surely this characteristic habit of using the same symbol to represent such a vast range of experiences must be one of the reasons why mathematics is so difficult for many students.

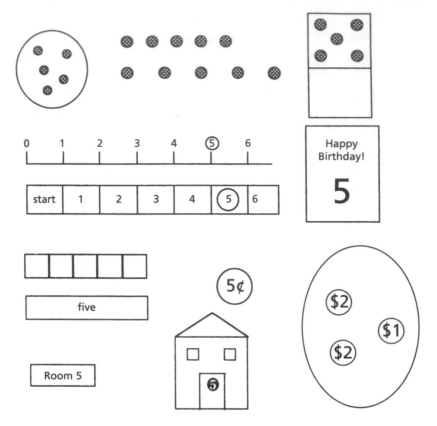

FIGURE 3.1 *Some experiences of "five"*

The teaching of mathematics is too often done without reference to the concrete experiences which the mathematics is supposed to make more meaningful. This only makes both the mathematics and the concrete experiences more inaccessible. Teachers often take these connections for granted because they are so natural for us adults. However, low-achieving students may not have had the opportunity to make these connections and see these relationships in an important way. A major challenge for the teacher, therefore, is to see this need and then to help the student make the connections between the manipulations of the symbols and the corresponding concrete experiences. Make sample charts or problems available, including the meaning of mathematical symbols, special terms, and procedures for using a calculator. These can be posted around the room or kept in notebooks. Teachers can also use visuals, manipulatives, and real objects when presenting and reinforcing mathematical ideas. Beginning with something too abstract can confuse students.

Teaching concepts well can be challenging. It is important to know what the students already understand before trying something more complex or different. Explicitly define the concepts and have many examples available, particularly examples of things that are not the concept in question in order to show boundaries and distinctions. Visual cues of boxes, pointers, and color coding will highlight the salient attributes and characteristics of the concepts in question, helping students focus their attention.

We will use the concept of a set of 5 things to illustrate. Set out many examples of sets of five things: trees, marbles, spoons, children, etc. To show the boundaries of the concept, use close examples: four trees, six children, etc. This helps students to key on the critical attributes of the concept and to avoid classifying errors. This approach is also effective with more complex concepts, such as "zero" which we will explain in Chapter 4 on place value.

Unstable truths and models

A surprising feature of mathematical experience is that children may often learn "truths" and develop models early on that later have to be unlearned or modified as their experiences of number widen. For example, they may learn to think of a number as a set of things, a model constantly reinforced by the majority of concrete examples used by their teachers. Later, they cannot make any sense of negative numbers which cannot be interpreted as sets of things, because the idea of a number as a label for ordering is not a major part of their understanding. They may learn to say things like "three take away five, can't be done . . . ," only to be told later that you *can* do it and the answer is "–2." They pick up the ideas that subtraction makes things smaller and multiplication makes things bigger, and are confounded when they meet "6 – (–2) = 8," "75 x 0.2 = 15," and "1/2 ÷ 1/2 = 1." This phenomenon is not peculiar to learning mathematics, of course. The concept we develop through our early experiences of what constitutes a "foreigner," for example, has to be modified radically when we travel abroad and discover that we are now the foreigners. But when this happens in mathematics, where we are conditioned to think that what is right and what is wrong is always clear cut, it can undermine the confidence of the poor student struggling to make sense of it. (For a fuller discussion of this and the issues raised in the previous two sections, refer to Haylock and Cockburn (1997).)

Mathematical ideas need to be learned and then unlearned or modified as the experiences of the learners progress.

To guard against this problem, teachers can focus on process and mathematical understandings which will later become the basis of revised student thinking. By using purposeful tasks in meaningful contexts that make students think, teachers can help students to form more accurate and enduring understandings of mathematical concepts.

Complex language patterns

A mathematical statement which we might expect a young child to formulate would be: "seven is two more than five"; or its equivalent, "five is two less than seven." These are typical of the complex language patterns that are peculiar to mathematics and do not come easily to many children. They may need specific help to establish some of these language patterns in their talking and writing repertoire. To make statements of this kind or to understand many of the instructions in mathematics textbooks or activity cards, children must hold a number of abstract concepts in their minds and be able to relate them.

Mathematical language is very complex, a fact we often take for granted.

A question for 10- to 11-year-olds, taken from an elementary mathematics curriculum, reads: "Which number between 25 and 30 cannot be divided exactly by either 2 or 3?" Students might be able to read and understand each individual word in this question, but together they form a complex intellectual task. The children must hold in their minds that the task requires the identification of one number; that to find this number, each number greater than 25 but less than 30 must be tested; and that the test must determine firstly whether the number is divisible by 2, secondly whether it is divisible by 3, and then reject it if either is the case. They must be able to call to mind the procedures for testing for divisibility by 2 and by 3, while remembering which numbers have been tested and which have passed or failed which tests, and all the time retaining the aim of the task. This is typical of the level of intellectual demand in many apparently simple mathematical statements, questions, or instructions. Many children with experience of only a limited range of language structures and vocabulary in their everyday lives will need help with some of the key words required to communicate mathematical ideas: words such as "either," "each," "altogether," and "between," which appear infrequently in their normal conversation. They will need help in clarifying the subtle differences in meaning implied by different prepositions such as sharing "with" and sharing "among." The formation of sentences such as "18 shared among 6 is 3 each" and "6 sets of 3 makes 18 altogether" is a major difficulty for many students, but is an essential component in their learning of mathematics. To help students make these distinctions and relate the words to the activity, techniques for teaching concepts, introduced earlier in this chapter, would prove helpful. Use plenty of examples and contrast these with situations that do not fit. Have students compare and contrast various actions and wordings so that the critical attributes become firmly understood.

The overuse of the text

Most elementary and middle schools invest a considerable amount of their budget in their mathematics program. This might consist of boxes of activity cards, a series of workbooks, or a set of textbooks, often with the expectation that one box of cards or one set of books will determine the mathematics curriculum for one year of schooling. It is interesting to note that there is more reliance on commercially produced programs for teaching mathematics than for any other subject in the curriculum, although this is gradually changing. In a subject where many teachers are traditionally lacking in confidence themselves, the program or textbook series provides them with security, ready-made decisions about the order and quantity of various mathematical exercises and experiences, some confidence about what the children will have done already, and enough activities to keep children occupied in mathematics for the four or five hours a week allotted on the timetable. An author of a mathematics program, who has never met the children concerned, cannot, of course, determine exactly what mathematical activities, in what order, and in what quantity, should be given to each and every individual in the class.

Too often the program or textbook, instead of the particular needs of the students, drives the mathematics instruction in a classroom.

Almost inevitably, a textbook on its own, usually produced with average and above-average students in mind, provides an inappropriate curriculum for our low achievers in mathematics. Teachers concerned about doing the best for these students must be prepared to view the program as a resource to be used and not a master to be obeyed. We feel that prescribed lessons can be supplemented with activities of the teachers' own devising or taken from other sources, based on their knowledge of the particular difficulties and characteristics of each individual they teach. Learning mathematics, especially for the low-achieving students, must not be perceived as simply getting through the program. We are convinced that this is a serious shortcoming in the teaching of mathematics and contributes to the lack of progress of many students.

Individualized learning

A misguided reliance on individualized learning as a teaching approach for mathematics has become very common in elementary schools in recent years. In this programmed learning approach, each child spends most mathematics lessons working individually, at his or her own pace, through a series of activity cards or pages of a workbook. When a card or page is completed they get it marked and then either do their corrections or go on to the next card or page. Sometimes they do the marking themselves using the answer sheet provided, but more often they join a line of students at the teacher's desk. If they have problems with a task they must either signal for the teacher's attention or join the lineup.

Individualized learning in a rigid program often deprives students of the opportunity to do mathematics and to verbalize their new understandings with others.

Again, it is quite understandable why some teachers have opted for such an approach. In a mixed-ability class, the range of competence and rate of progress in mathematics is so enormous that there seem to be many advantages in allowing students to progress at their own speeds. Even in schools where classes are grouped for mathematics, the range of ability in the bottom (and, incidentally, the top) groups will be considerable and probably greater than those in the middle groups. This is simply a statistical consequence of the way in which human attributes (height, weight, life-span, IQ, mathematics achievement, etc.) tend to be distributed, with most people clustered around the average and fewer people falling in the extremes.

To cope with this range of achievement, many teachers have turned to individualized learning programs. However, there are many potential difficulties with this approach. Our observations of mathematics lessons in many schools convince us that an unquestioning reliance on this method of organizing students' learning experiences in mathematics is often disastrous for many children, particularly low achievers.

As we argued in the previous chapter, one basic mistake is that this approach relies on the written word as the medium of instruction. The best way for most low achievers to come to understand many mathematical ideas and processes is for someone to explain them orally, and the worst way is to rely on their generally poor reading skills. In many classes where the individualized learning approach is used, students receive little direct instruction from the teacher. With twenty-five students working on twenty-five different tasks, the teacher becomes little more than a marking machine, frantically trying to keep the line at the desk to a manageable size. In an hour's lesson any given child cannot expect more than two minutes of the teacher's time on average. Instruction from the teacher is only in response to a difficulty with a card and is inevitably almost entirely procedural, that is, telling the child what they have to do in order to comply with the demands of the card in question. During a one-hour lesson using this approach, Derek observed that a typical student spent only twelve minutes working on mathematics and the rest of the time doing nothing because the student was stuck on a problem, waiting, chatting to friends, wandering round the room, organizing his desk, looking for materials, and so on.

Sometimes we have even come across children who, when they come to a card requiring some materials for practical work, such as jugs of water or weighing scales, tell us that their teacher has told them to skip these cards. This policy is probably adopted because, with each child working individually, the teacher is unable to predict the need for practical materials in any given lesson. Given the fundamental importance of practical experience in mathematics, particularly in elementary school, such a policy is clearly less than ideal.

Mathematics educators generally agree that discussion — both between students and between teachers and students — is an important component of good mathematics teaching. By trying to articulate their mathematical ideas, children clarify their concepts and gain mastery of the language patterns of mathematics. The individualized learning approach provides little opportunity for such discussion. A report on the special needs of girls learning mathematics (Royal Society and IMA, 1986) emphasizes the importance of encouraging girls to talk about mathematics and to listen to each other, so as to bring a "social" element to the teaching.

To some extent, the picture we paint of the individualized learning approach may be a caricature. We know many teachers who use variations of this approach skilfully and effectively, organizing the tasks and resources in ways which allow opportunities for instruction, explanation, discussion, and practical work. Some teachers employ this method for half the mathematics lessons in a week and adopt different organizational approaches, such as whole-class or small-group activities, for the others. And, of course, problems and compromises are involved in any method of organizing students' learning activities in a large class. But we know that the programmed or individualized mathematics lesson described above is all too common, and our conviction, based on the observation of many such lessons, is that such an approach is a major contributory factor in the lack of progress many children experience in mathematics.

Drill and Practice

There are basic mathematical skills that need to be mastered and, from time to time, routine practice of these is essential for all students. It is particularly helpful when working with low achievers to specify precise, short-term targets for the learning of such basic skills, so that those who have experienced repeated failure in this subject can recognize that they are actually making progress. Learning targets need to be clear and detailed but also realistic and relevant to the actual needs of the students. Short games and puzzles often provide more interesting contexts for mastering mathematical skills and competencies than pages of worksheets and hours of flashcards.

Key teaching points

- Help students achieve a sense of accomplishment
- Focus more on the process and not just the final "answer"
- Occasionally use problems with no clear or correct answers
- Use purposeful, thought-provoking tasks
- Ensure a degree of mastery of foundational skills and understandings before moving on
- Heighten a sense of intrigue and arouse curiosity in students
- Use a variety of cues at the same time: auditory, visual, tactile, memory
- Post sample charts and problems around the room
- Use visuals, manipulatives, and real things (when possible)
- Teach concepts thoroughly: use plenty of examples and counter-examples
- Customize the mathematics program according to the needs of the students
- Avoid overuse of individualized programs; always provide direct teacher instruction and explanations, opportunities for discussion with peers, and practical work
- For drill and practice, use short-term, self-referenced student goals and interesting contexts

QUESTIONS FOR DISCUSSION WITH COLLEAGUES

1. Does our description of school mathematics seem to match your perceptions?
2. In what ways does your program differ from the mathematics commonly taught in schools today?
3. Which of the teaching suggestions outlined in this chapter might you try? Why?

4
Place Value

FEATURES OF THIS CHAPTER

- important elements of the place-value system
- key considerations in teaching place value
- specific learning targets for low achievers (cross-referenced to activities)
- activities for students (cross-referenced to targets)
- key teaching points

Important elements of the place-value system

Derek once encountered a Grade 6 student who wrote "10064" for "one hundred sixty-four." This revealed that the student had not yet mastered the essential principle on which our number system is based, that of place value, and therefore wrote "100" as an abbreviation for "one hundred" and then "64" for "sixty-four." In our number system, part of the meaning of each symbol is determined by the place where it is written in relation to other symbols. Place value is a highly sophisticated and powerful system, enabling us to express large numbers in a concise form without the need to invent further symbols.

The whole modern world is indebted to the Indian and Arabic cultures for a number system which made most of the mathematical, scientific, and technological developments of the last thousand years possible.

When we compare the numeral "888" with its Roman numeral equivalent, "DCCCLXXXVIII," we notice that although both numerals represent the same number, the first version is much more compact, more easily interpreted, more readily compared with other numbers, and more amenable to arithmetic manipulations than the second.

Helping our students make the correct connections between the words and the symbols for numbers is a major part of the task of developing their understanding of place value.

The basic components of this number system are:
- a set of digits (symbols): 0, 1, 2, 3, 4, 5, 6, 7, 8, 9;
- the base of the number system, i.e., "ten";
- powers of the base: ones, tens, hundreds, thousands, ten thousands, and so on;
- the places in which the digits are written; and
- certain conventions about the way the numbers are read.

> We often take the very complex features of the place-value system for granted because they are so automatic for us.

The power of "place"

> Some low achievers may not yet have deciphered the complex place-value system. We need to give them opportunities to think about what our number system means.

Our place-value system has many conventions which gives it great power and elegance. We can see how the components of the number system contribute to the meaning of, for example, the numeral "453." As we work from right to left (not the conventional direction for reading, of course), the places of the digits represent consecutive powers of the base. The digits "3," "5," and "4" mean that we have "three ones," "five tens," and "four hundreds." These powers are connected by the simple, recurring principle that "one of these is ten of those": one ten is ten ones, one hundred is ten tens, one thousand is ten hundreds, and so on.

Although we work from right to left in determining the place values, by convention we actually read the number from left to right, giving the largest place-value digits first. Our number is "four hundreds, five tens, three ones." There are further conventions: we abbreviate the "four hundreds" to "four hundred," the "five tens" to "fifty," and the "three ones" to "three," and we do not use the word "and" (except in expressing decimal fractions such as 2.1 when read as "2 and one tenth"). Numbers which have 11, 12, 13, 14, 15, 16, 17, 18, or 19 as the last two digits are exceptions to these rules. So finally we read the number as "four hundred fifty-three." You may want to retain the use of "and" to be consistent with local practices. Thus 453 would read "four hundred and fifty three."

Zero

Students have many difficulties with "zero" both in how to interpret it and in how to handle it in calculations. Some find it hard to accept that zero is actually a number, since it is often referred to as "nothing." In many situations, zero does represent "nothing." For example, if the number of objects in a box is "zero," the box is empty; there is literally nothing in it. If an article is priced at zero dollars, then it costs nothing. But when zero is used in its ordinal sense as a label on a number line, then it definitely does not mean "nothing." For example, a temperature of zero degrees does not mean there is no temperature, and a location does not cease to exist if its elevation is zero m above sea level.

It is important, therefore, that students gain experience of using zero in a wide range

> Zero does not always mean "nothing," although it does have this meaning when it operates as a place holder in our numeration system.

of practical contexts, both those where it represents nothing (describing an empty set of things) and those where it represents a position on an ordinal scale (a point on a number line or thermometer).

In fact, the function of zero in the place-value system is to indicate that a place has "nothing." For example, in the numeral 604 the zero indicates that the tens place is empty; there is nothing in it. This is an important component to understanding the place-value system. We need the zero digit in the empty place in order to recognize that the other digits represent hundreds and ones. When students read the numeral they have to learn to skip the place occupied by the zero, and say "six hundred four".

It is important that students learn that it is the *position* of the 6 that leads one to say "six hundred," not the zero that follows it. So, for example, in the numeral "400," the position of the "4" indicates that the 4 is in the hundreds place, not the "00" following it. The two zeros simply serve to indicate that the "4" is actually in the hundreds place and that there are no tens and no ones. We can see how this leads to the confused child who writes "10064" when she means "164": she interprets the "00" as signaling the word "hundred" rather than two empty places.

Differentiating among zero's various meanings and learning to use zero as a place holder can be done using the guidelines for developing an understanding of concepts, introduced in Chapter 3. First, tell students that zero can mean "nothing" or an empty set of things. Then show plenty of diverse examples such as an empty box, an empty measuring cup, an empty bank account. Do not, for instance, use only examples of empty boxes or only no money as this will cue the incorrect attribute of box or money. Then, provide examples of instances where zero actually represents something, as in temperature (students who experience winter may have an easier time with this) or in elevation.

To help students learn that zero in the place-value system means nothing and also holds a place, introduce many examples again. Relate the numerals to base-ten blocks. Show 20, 30, etc. using blocks and point out that the ones place is empty. The empty place is shown by placing a zero there which allows us to know that the other digit is in the tens place. Contrast these examples with single digit numerals and ask students to tell you why they are not twenty, thirty, or forty, etc. When these are mastered, move on to hundreds. Show 400, 500, 600, and so on using base-ten blocks and the numeral for them. Point out that the zeros correspond to the empty sets in the tens and ones places. Contrast these numerals with single and double digits and ask the students to explain why they do not represent hundreds. By working with many examples and counter-examples, students will begin to distinguish among the various concepts and will learn to use them confidently in the place-value system.

The principle of exchange

The principle that "one of these is ten of those," as we move left to right from one place to the next in a numeral (and its equivalent, "ten of these is one of those" as we move from right to left), is at the heart of our number system. We use this phrase frequently when helping students understand the procedures of arithmetic. Whenever we get ten of one sort (when, for example, we are adding two numbers) we can exchange them for one of the next sort (i.e., "carry one"), going from right to left. Similarly, when we need to, we can always exchange one of one sort for ten of the next (for example, when using the decomposition algorithm for subtraction), going from left to right. This principle is a key to addition and subtraction operations with exchanges.

Practical experience of this principle of exchanging one for ten (or ten for one) should form a major component in the development of understanding of place value. It can be wonderfully demonstrated using base-ten blocks and coins. For example, one dime can be exchanged for 10 pennies and a one-dollar-coin or bill can be exchanged for 10 dimes.

Key considerations in teaching place value

Several approaches are shown here to address the many crucial points about teaching place value to low achievers.

Connections

One of the most powerful representations of number is a number line. Its spatial imagery is particularly helpful in developing the skill of ordering applied to numbers as in "greater than," "less than," and "between."

> Students can make important connections between the words and symbols for numbers and pictures of numbers on the number line.

The ability to order a set of numbers at sight is an important component of mastery of the place-value system. To do this, we must first recognize that, for example, any four-digit whole number or integer must automatically be greater than any three-digit number. Next, when comparing two numbers with the same number of digits, we have to learn that the most significant digit is the one on the left, and that the digits become less significant as we move from left to right. This concept is also applicable to an understanding of decimal fractions, so learning it early will establish a sound foundation for later extensions.

Learning to position numbers on a number line labeled in hundreds, for example, can help a student develop an understanding of place value, since it reinforces these procedures for ordering and gives them a spatial interpretation.

Teaching for transfer

Building up connections between concrete materials and the language and symbols of numbers is also crucial to developing sound understandings of place value and for transfer of learning. The multi-embodiment principle (also called the perceptual variability principle), enunciated by the influential mathematics educator, Zoltan Dienes (see, for example, Dienes, 1960) is particularly helpful.

> The more models or embodiments of the same mathematical idea that students encounter with success, the more secure and robust is their understanding.

Dienes suggests that our understanding of an abstract mathematical concept or principle is more secure if we experience it in a variety of concrete embodiments. Our students will benefit from more than one embodiment or model of the principle and from specific help in making the connections. This is consistent with the research on concept attainment, in which numerous examples and counter-examples help students to formulate a concept correctly (Bruner et al., 1967; Tennyson & Park, 1980).

We need sets of concrete materials which embody the "one of these is ten of those" idea. Some materials developed by Dienes are the base-ten blocks shown in Figure 4.1.

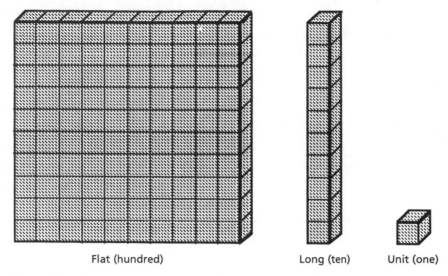

Flat (hundred)   Long (ten)   Unit (one)

FIGURE 4.1 *Dienes's Base-Ten Blocks. The "exchange principle" means simply that one long can be made from ten units and one flat from ten longs.*

The same principle can be experienced with money, both length and mass in the metric system, and the abacus, giving us five possible models to use when teaching place value (up to three-digit numbers only):

- *base-ten blocks:* units, longs, flats
- *coins:* pennies, dimes, and dollars
- *rods:* centimeters, decimeters, meters
- *mass:* one-gram masses, ten-gram masses, hundred-gram masses
- *an abacus:* using different colored counters on pegs to represent ones, tens, and hundreds

Each model provides a concrete situation in which the principle of exchanging ten of one sort for one of another operates. With the blocks, the students can see that "one of these is ten of those," since one piece can actually be made from ten smaller pieces fit together. When working with coins or play money, the principle is a little more abstract: "one of these is worth ten of those." Theoretically one would expect this to be more difficult to grasp, but in practice we find that most students in the 8 to 12 age range have enough experience with money in their lives outside of school to handle this principle of exchange quite confidently. In fact, of all the suggestions we have ever made to those who teach mathematics to low achievers, the simple idea of doing number work practically with coins or play money, using just pennies, dimes, and dollars, has proved to be the most helpful. Incidentally, when using coins, we switch quite freely between referring to a dollar coin or bill as "a dollar" ($1.00) and calling it "a hundred" (100 cents) — and we keep on stressing that "one of these is worth ten of those" (i.e., ten of the dimes).

> Base-ten blocks and coins or play money are the most effective materials to help students understand place value.

By contrast, many low-achieving students have difficulties handling the less familiar concepts of metric length and mass, so these models are less useful for experiencing the concept of place value. Therefore, establish mathematical structures first in contexts that are more familiar to students (such as handling money) and then move these structures into less familiar contexts (such as handling metric lengths and masses or using the abacus).

A note on money notation

When working with coins, students will learn to connect, for example, "4 dollars, 5 dimes and 3 cents" with the number "453": they must recognize that they have the equivalent of 453 cents. But they will also encounter situations where this sum of money is written "$4.53." Students have to be taught this convention of always writing two digits after the decimal point when writing sums of money using the dollar sign, the first digit indicating the number of dimes, the second the number of pennies. This is, in fact, a useful introduction to the use of decimal notation, arising quite naturally from the student's own experience of prices and shopping. Therefore, we should ensure that students can translate freely between these two ways of representing a sum of money.

Zero poses other challenges in translating, since 50 cents can be written 50¢ or $0.50 and 5 cents can be written 5¢ or $0.05.

There are other potential problems, discovered when students are doing calculations with money on their calculators. For example, use a calculator to find:

- the cost of 6 pens at $1.45 each
- the cost per battery if a pack of three costs $2.95

For the first problem, you enter "1.45 x 6" and the calculator displays the result "8.7." One obvious interpretation is that 8.7 represents eight dollars and seven cents. Similarly, the second case gives the answer 0.9833333; how does the student deal with that? We explain to them that the calculator does not know that you must have two and only two digits after the decimal point when you calculate money. So in one case we have to put the second digit in ourselves (8.70), and in the other case (0.98) we have to throw away the extra digits. (Explain that the discarded digits represent little bits of money worth less than a penny.)

Students will need guidance interpreting calculator displays such as 8.7 (meaning $8.70) and 0.98333333 (meaning $0.98).

Specific learning targets for low achievers

Having considered what is involved in understanding this important principle of place value, we now propose a set of realistic and attainable learning targets for 8 to 12-year-old low achievers. These targets might also be appropriate for younger or older students. Many targets focus on behaviors which show that the student has formed significant connections between language, symbols, the number line, and the two concrete embodiments (base-ten blocks and coins). The targets are consistent with NCTM *Curriculum and Evaluation Standards* which state that students should be able to "construct number meanings

Realistic and Attainable Targets → Relevant and Purposeful Activities → Appropriate Assessment

through real-world experiences and the use of physical materials and understand our numeration system by relating counting, grouping, and place-value concepts" (NCTM, 1989, p. 38).

We have framed these targets mainly with three-digit whole numbers in mind. For many of our low achievers up to the age of 12 years, mastery of three-digit numbers is a sufficient goal, particularly since they rarely need to use numbers greater than a thousand in their day-to-day lives. If they can achieve these targets with three-digit numbers, then we feel confident that they have sufficient understanding of the place-value principle to extend it to four or more places. (Some targets related to handling big numbers are included in Chapter 6.)

When working toward these place-value targets, you might want to specify similar targets with two-digit numbers first. Most of the targets are easily modified to two- or four-digit numbers, although the use of coins becomes inappropriate beyond three digits. Instead, you would have to use play money with bills of larger denominations.

Each target should be specific enough to make its assessment clear. In some cases, however, we clarify this with examples. Remember that some assessment tasks, which can justifiably be criticized as having little connection with real life, may give a less than fair indication of true understanding. You may find that students can better demonstrate their understanding by their performance in some of the activities given later in the chapter, where the same mathematical tasks are embedded in more purposeful and relevant place-value games.

A set of 25 targets for place value is given below. If we can get our low achievers to succeed on this limited set of targets, then we will have given them a solid foundation of understanding for further development of numeracy.

Place-value Targets 1 to 4

The student should be able:

These targets focus on the principle of exchange, using coins and base-ten blocks.

1. Given a pile of one-cent coins (less than a hundred), to reduce this to the smallest number of equivalent coins, using a process of exchange. For example, given a pile of 67 pennies and a supply of dimes, the student should be able to reduce the pile of pennies to 6 dimes and 7 pennies, by exchanging 10 ones at a time for a ten.

See Activities 4.1, 4.2, and 4.3.

2. Given a pile of base-ten units (less than a hundred), to reduce this to the smallest number of equivalent blocks, using a process of exchange. For example, given a pile of 43 units and a supply of longs, the student should be able to reduce the pile of units to 4 longs and 3 units, by exchanging ten units at a time for a long.

3. Given a pile of one-cent and 10-cent coins, to reduce this to the smallest number of equivalent coins, using a process of exchange. For example, with a supply of pennies, dimes, and one-dollar coins or bills, the student should be able to reduce a pile of 28 dimes and 35 pennies to 3 one-dollar coins or bills, 1 dime, and 5 pennies.)

4. Given a pile of base-ten units and longs (less than the equivalent of a thousand units), to reduce this to the smallest number of equivalent flats, using a process of exchange. Similar to Target 3: a supply of longs and hundreds flats should be available for exchange.

Place-value Targets 5 to 11

Ensure that these targets are attained, particularly for frequently confused numbers such as 471 and 417 or 417 and 470. The student should also be able to handle numbers with 0 in either the tens or the units place, or with 11, 12, 13, 14, 15, 16, 17, 18, or 19 as the last two digits.

> Targets 5 to 11 highlight the connections among symbols, language, and concrete materials. See Figure 2.1.

For all possible three-digit numbers, then, the student should be able:

5. To say in words the name of any written three-digit numeral. (For example, the student should be able to say the names of 278, 465, 564, 103, 130, 405, 450, 471, 417, 470, 600, 812, etc.)

6. To write the numeral for any stated three-digit number. (This is the reverse of Target 5: here the number is stated in words and the student writes the corresponding numeral.

> See Activities 4.4, 4.5, 4.6, 4.7, and 4.14.

7. To demonstrate the meaning of the digits in a three-digit numeral by selecting appropriate items from a supply of pennies, dimes, and one-dollar coins or bills. (For example, the student should be able to show the number "403" by selecting 4 one-dollar coins or bills and 3 pennies.)

8. To demonstrate the meaning of the digits in a three-digit numeral by selecting appropriate blocks from a supply of base-ten materials (units, longs, and flats).

9. Given a collection of items (pennies, dimes, and one-dollar coins or bills: no more than nine of each), to say and write the corresponding number.

10. Given a collection of base-ten blocks (units, longs, flats: no more than nine of each), to say and write the corresponding number.

When these targets have been attained, the student should then be able:

11. To explain the meaning of each digit in a three-digit number. (For example, explain that the "4" in "453" represents "4 hundreds," the "5" represents "5 tens," and the "3" represent "3 ones." Examples with zeros are particularly significant in this target.)

Place-value Targets 12 to 15

As with Targets 5 to 11, it is important that the student attain these targets for the full range of three-digit numbers, particularly those which give rise to common misunderstandings and confusions. The student should be able:

> These targets apply to the connections between the picture of number in the number line and the language and symbols of number.

12. To indicate the approximate position of a three-digit number, given in words or symbols, on an appropriate section of a number line marked in tens. (For example, the student should be able to indicate the approximate positions of 305, 352, 399 on the number line shown in Figure 4.2(a).)

(a)

280 290 300 310 320 330 340 350 360 370 380 390 400 410

(b)

0 100 200 300 400 500 600 700 800 900 1000 1100 1200 1300

(c)

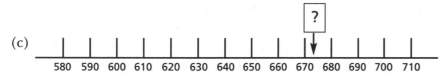

?

580 590 600 610 620 630 640 650 660 670 680 690 700 710

(d)

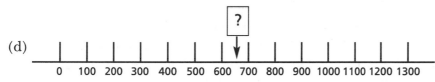

?

0 100 200 300 400 500 600 700 800 900 1000 1100 1200 1300

FIGURE 4.2 *Connecting numerals with number line diagrams*

13. To indicate the approximate position of a three-digit number, given in words or symbols, on a number line marked in hundreds. (For example, the student should be able to indicate the approximate positions of 305, 450, 790 on the number line shown in Figure 4.2(b).)

14. To state the approximate number corresponding to a given point on a number line labeled in tens. (For example, to recognize that the arrow in Figure 4.2(c) is pointing to 673 or close to that.)

15. To state the approximate number corresponding to a given point on a number line labeled in hundreds. (For example, to recognize that the arrow in Figure 4.2(d) is pointing to about 660.)

Place-value Targets 16 and 17

The student should be able:

16. To arrange a set of numbers (up to 999) in order (a) from smallest to largest and (b) from largest to smallest.

17. To write a number which comes between two given numbers (up to 999).

These targets focus on the application of the place-value principle to the processes of ordering numbers.

See Activities 4.7 and 4.11.

Place-value Targets 18 to 21

Students' understanding of place value can be shown by the ease with which they can single out the hundreds, the tens, or the ones in a number in mental arithmetic. These targets, which can specifically indicate the students' understanding of place value, are extended in Chapter 7.

These four targets focus simply on the ability to add or subtract 1, 10, 100, 2, 20, or 200 mentally.

To show that they can mentally choose the appropriate place in a three-digit number, the student should be able:

See Activities 4.8, 4.9, and 4.10.

18. To add 1, 10, or 100 mentally to any given three-digit number (especially examples containing the digit 9, e.g., add 10 to 796).

19. To subtract 1, 10, or 100 mentally from any given three-digit number (especially examples containing the digit 0, e.g., subtract 10 from 804).

20. To add 2, 20, or 200 mentally to any given three-digit number (especially examples containing the digits 8 or 9, e.g., add 20 to 386).

21. To subtract 2, 20, or 200 mentally from any given three-digit number (especially examples containing the digits 0 or 1, e.g., to subtract 20 from 406).

Place-value Targets 22 to 25

These four targets show that the student can use the process of exchange in the contexts of addition and subtraction.

When adding and subtracting, we encounter the need for the process of exchange which lies at the heart of the understanding of place value. Since this is a target for understanding place value, and not one related to the ability to perform calculations, we are looking here for no more than the ability to use the process of exchange in adding and subtracting with concrete materials. Therefore, the student should be able:

See Activities 4.12 and 4.13.

22. To perform an addition of two three-digit numbers by setting out the corresponding two sets of coins (pennies, dimes, and one-dollar coins or bills), combining them, exchanging where necessary, and stating the answer with economy of coins.

23. To perform an addition of two three-digit numbers by putting out the corresponding two sets of base-ten blocks, combining them, exchanging where necessary, and stating the answer with economy of blocks.

24. To perform a subtraction with two three-digit numbers by putting out the set of coins corresponding to the larger number, taking away the set corresponding to the smaller number, exchanging where necessary, and stating the answer with economy of coins. (For example, given "413 – 275," the student would put out 4 one-dollar coins or bills, 1 dime, and 3 pennies. They would then exchange the dime for 10 pennies and take away the required 5 pennies, exchange one of the dollar coins for 10 dimes and take away the required 7 dimes, and then take away the required 2 dollar coins. This would leave them with 1 dollar coin, 3 dimes, and 8 pennies, which they would interpret as the answer "138¢." This process is known formally as subtraction by decomposition.)

25. To perform a subtraction with two three-digit numbers by putting out the corresponding set of base-ten blocks for the larger number, taking away the set corresponding to the smaller number, exchanging where necessary, and stating the answer.

Place-value Targets 26 to 31, related to money

It is important to include in our work with low achievers some additional targets related to the specific problems of money notation, allowing us to extend the principles of place

Targets
26 to 31 stress
the challenge of
money notation.

value to this first important experience of decimal notation. The targets include being able to translate freely between the cent notation (235¢) and the dollar notation ($2.35) and to use the conventions for the latter correctly (e.g., two figures after the point and no

See
Activities 4.11,
4.15, and 4.16.

"¢" sign). Design activities to ensure that the students are able:

26. To write a sum of money given in cents correctly with a dollar sign and vice versa. (Include translating, for example, between 25¢ and $0.25, and between 7¢ and $0.07.)

27. Given a collection of coins (pennies, dimes, and one-dollar coins or bills, no more than nine of each), to write down the sum of money using the dollar notation.

28. Given a sum of money using the dollar notation, to put out the corresponding collection of coins.

29. To interpret correctly the sum of money indicated by an answer to a calculation performed on a calculator (for example, calculator answers such as 8.3, which has to be interpreted as $8.30, and 8.6666666, which has to be interpreted as $8.66. Note: we do not include a requirement for rounding to the nearest digit as a realistic or necessary target for low achievers in this age range when learning place value.)

30. To arrange a set of prices, written in dollar notation, in order from (a) lowest to highest and (b) highest to lowest (for example, to order these prices: $4.50, $4.99, $4.05, $5.00, $0.75, and $3.10.)

31. To write down a sum of money which comes between two given sums of money, expressed in dollar notation. (For example, to write down an amount between $5.99 and $6.10.)

Suggested activities

All these games[1] have been used successfully with low achievers, and are, in our experience, more effective for developing understanding and in generating commitment than most workbooks and textbook exercises.

We
encourage you to modify
these games and tasks for
your own situations and,
whenever possible, to involve
students in the creation of
games and activities.

Materials and methods are outlined for each activity. The variations provided are only examples to alert you to some of the possibilities. The targets for each activity are listed, and those addressed by the suggested variations are given in parentheses.

Generating numbers at random

A number of the activities suggested here (and in later chapters) make use of packs of homemade cards as a means of generating numbers at random. Good-quality blank playing cards can be obtained from educational suppliers. It is probably worth the time and expense to prepare some attractive sets of these cards: children seem to be more motivated by good-quality cards than by those cut from old cereal boxes. To start with, prepare:

---

[1]Only Activity 4.16 has not specifically been tested with low achievers.

- Pack A: 50 red cards, five each with one of the digits 0, 1, 2, 3, 4, 5, 6, 7, 8, 9, written on one side
- Pack B: 50 blue cards, five each with one of the digits 0, 1, 2, 3, 4, 5, 6, 7, 8, 9, written on one side.

Pack A is used as a simple means of generating single-digit numbers at random for various games. Pack A and Pack B used together can generate two-digit numbers at random, with, say, the blue cards representing tens and the red cards representing ones. We prefer cards to various kinds of dice for generating numbers at random for small-group games, simply because dealing cards is quieter and less likely to be disruptive in a classroom.

If dice are used, note that ten-faced dice, numbered from 0 to 9, are available from educational suppliers or game stores. Alternatively, wooden or plastic cubes with single digits written on them can be used: for example, a blue cube with the digits 1, 2, 4, 5, 6, 9 (representing tens) and a red cube with the digits 0, 3, 5, 7, 8, 9 (representing ones) will generate a good range of two-digit numbers.

Another alternative (which may appeal to many children) is to use a computer program to generate random numbers.

Activity 4.1 What's My Value

Targets 1 to 4: structured discovery of the exchange principle.

Materials
Base-ten blocks and coins; a chart of ones, tens, and hundreds.

Method
Students can be given the base-ten blocks, a small sampling of each size, and instructed to take the long, for example, and build an equivalent long with units. "How many does it take?" "How many longs does it take to make up a flat?" "How many units does it take to make up a flat?" Record the observations on a chart showing hundreds, tens, and ones. Students can then be given a selection of coins and asked the same questions. Record their observations. They may notice that the penny is like the single small cube because they both represent one unit, that the long and the dime are alike since they both represent 10 of the next smaller units, and so on.

Variations
When the students are ready, expand the chart to include other concrete embodiments of place value such as metric rods and weights and the abacus.

Activity 4.2 Race to a Dollar

This is a small-group game for up to four players plus a banker. It is one version of a fairly common game, which we regard as an essential experience of handling the basic place-value principle.

Target 1 (2): The principle of exchange.

Materials
Pack A (or some other means of generating single-digit numbers) and a supply of one-cent and 10-cent coins.

Method

The pack of cards is shuffled and placed face down in the middle of the table. Each player turns over a card, in turn. The number revealed indicates their winnings, which are paid to them in pennies by the banker. Used cards are placed face up on the table, then shuffled and reused when the pack is used up.

When a player has ten cents, he or she must exchange them at the bank for a dime before taking another turn. If another player spots that this has not been done, the offending player must miss a turn. The banker also acts as referee. The first player to get ten dimes (i.e., a dollar) is the winner. It is not necessary to insist that they finish exactly on a dollar.

Variation

Exactly the same game can then be played with base-ten units, longs, and flats thus focusing on Target 2.

By insisting that each player keep watch over the coins of other players and not his or her own, the object of the game can be to see how long it takes for each player to get one dollar, rather than who finishes first, or the students could all aim for a designated amount of money, working as part of a small team.

Activity 4.3 Race to Ten Dollars

Materials

Pack A and Pack B (or some other means of generating two-digit numbers) and a supply of pennies, dimes, and one-dollar coins or bills.

> Target 3 (4): the principle of exchange and Target 22 (23): combining in addition.

Method

The rules are similar to the previous game. Now, however, they use two packs of cards, Pack A (representing ones) and Pack B (representing tens). Each player turning over one card from each stack in turn to generate two-digit numbers. The banker pays them the appropriate number of tens and ones from the bank.

When a player has ten pennies or ten dimes, he or she must exchange them at the bank for a dime or a dollar respectively, before taking another turn. As with the previous game, failure to exchange results in missing a turn. The first player to get ten dollars (or more) is the winner.

Variation

The identical game can be played with base-ten units, longs, and flats, thus focusing on Target 4 and, to some extent, Target 23.

This game can also be an exercise in team work.

Activity 4.4 Place-value Cards

In this simple activity, two children practice translating between symbols and words for numbers, helping them to learn to recognize, for example, that the 5 in 453 represents 50, and that zero is a place holder.

> Targets 5 and 6: connections among language, concrete materials and symbols.

Materials

A set of cards (see Figure 4.3) with the numerals, shown in the top half of the figure, written on one side and the corresponding words, shown in the bottom half of the figure, on the other. Notice that the cards with "0" and "00" on one side are blank on the other: this is to emphasize the place-holder function of zero.

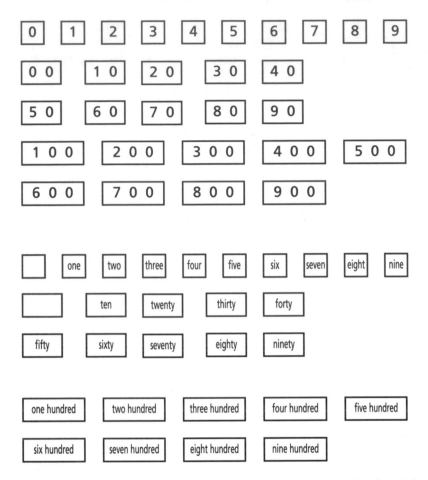

FIGURE 4.3 *Place-value cards (some teachers may want to include an "and" card. See discussion on p. 38)*

Method

The cards are arranged on the table, with the numerals face up, in three sets, single-digit numerals in one set, two-digit in the next, and three-digit in the next. One child picks up one card from each of the sets and assembles them, one on top of the other, to form a three-digit number. Say the cards 3, 50, and 400 are chosen, as in Figure 4.4(a). When they are placed one on top of the other, the number 453 emerges, as shown in Figure 4.4(b). This simple process shows very nicely how 453 is made up from 400, 50 and 3. The other student is then challenged to say the name of the number, and the cards are turned over and spread out as in Figure 4.4(c) to check whether this has been done correctly. Teachers may wish to include a recording element in the activity. For example, by copying the symbols and words written on the cards, the students might record the example as: "400 + 50 + 3 is the same as 453 is the same as four hundred fifty-three."

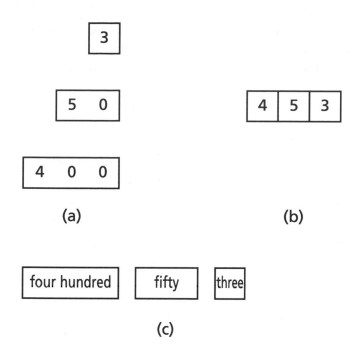

FIGURE 4.4 *Using the place-value cards*

Note: initially, remove the 10 (ten) card from the pack for this activity because of the special names used for numbers with a "1" in the tens position. When the children are confident with using the other cards, put the ten back in and discuss with the students the conventions for reading numbers like "417" (which appears as "four hundred ten seven" but is spoken as "four hundred seventeen").

Variation

The activity can then be done in reverse. Spread the cards out in rows with the words showing. One child chooses a three-digit number and writes it in symbols. Another child is challenged to select the cards required to assemble this number. For example, if one child writes "207," the other must pick up the card labeled "two hundred," the blank card from the two-digit row (because there are no tens), and the card labeled "seven." This child then turns over the cards to the digit side, places them one on top of the other, and confirms that they match the number written down.

Activity 4.5 Place-value Connections

Materials

Pack A, the place-value cards from Activity 4.4, a set of base-ten materials (units, longs, flats), and a set of coins (1 cent, 10 cent, 100 cent).

> Targets
> 7 to 10: connections among the numerals, the language, and the two concrete embodiments, coins and base-ten blocks.

Method

One child has Pack A, the second child has the place-value cards, the third child has the base-ten materials, and the fourth has the coins. Child 1 turns over three cards from Pack A to form a three-digit number. Child 2 assembles this number with the place-value cards and, turning them over, arranges the name of the number on the table. Child 3 puts out the corresponding blocks and Child 4 the corresponding coins. Child 1 checks that all the inputs are correct and then calls the teacher over to demonstrate the connections. After a few turns, the children move around one place in the sequence and become responsible for a different input.

Admittedly, this does not appear to be a very exciting activity, but it can be effective if used for short periods of about fifteen minutes, particularly with younger children. Encourage students to verbalize their connections among themselves and then with the teacher. They can take pride in being able to explain to the teacher how the numbers and representations are connected. You could call on them to defend their point of view. Some children will have the skills to write down their ideas.

Activity 4.6 Fish

Target 11:
connections among the numerals, the symbols, and the language.

Materials
A calculator for each player.

Method
This game is highly enjoyable provided the children can be trusted to cooperate with each other and play honestly. If players are required to write their number out on a card at the beginning of each round, then it can be checked at the end of the round.

Each player enters a three-digit number on their calculator. This is not revealed to other players. The game is then played like the traditional "Fish" card game, with players asking each other in turn whether they have particular digits, and being required to hand them over if they have.

The easiest way to explain the game is to give an example. Three players, X, Y, and Z, choose the numbers 453, 634, and 135 respectively. Player X starts the game.

X asks Y: "Have you any fives?"

Y (634) responds to X: "No." (End of X's turn.)

Y asks Z: "Have you any threes?"

Z (135) responds to Y: "Yes, three tens."

(Z now "gives" Y the three tens, i.e. Z subtracts 30 from his or her number and Y adds 30 to his or hers. Y now has 664 on display, Z has 105. Y, having been successful, gets another turn.)

Y asks X: "Have you any sixes?"

X (453) responds to Y: "No." (End of Y's turn.)

Z asks X: "Have you any threes?"

X (453) responds to Z: "Yes, three ones."

(X subtracts 3, leaving 450 on display; Z adds 3, getting 108 on display.)

Z asks Y: "Have you any sixes?"

Y (664) responds to Z: "Yes, six hundreds and six tens!"

(Y must now give both the 600 and the 60 to Z. So, Y subtracts 600 and 60 in turn from his or her number, leaving him or her with just 4 on display. Z adds 600 and 60 to his or her number, getting a total of 768. And so on.)

A player is out when his or her display is reduced to zero. The winning player should end up with the total of all the starting numbers. The players could then calculate the total as a check that the game has been played correctly.

An interesting feature of this game is the children's behavior when someone gets a total displayed greater than a thousand. Even low achievers catch on very quickly that asking "Have you any ones?" is a good tactic for getting a thousand off a player who has recently won a large number of hundreds. Once discovered, the thousand tends to get passed around very rapidly from player to player.

Activity 4.7 Boxes

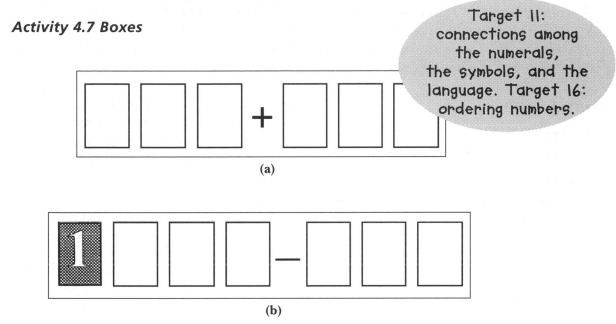

Target 11: connections among the numerals, the symbols, and the language. Target 16: ordering numbers.

(a)

(b)

FIGURE 4.5 *Boxes (for Activity 4.7)*

Materials

Pack A, a strip of cardstock with boxes drawn as shown in Figure 4.5(a) for each player (the boxes should be the same size as the cards in the pack), and a calculator for each player.

Method

In turn, each player turns over a card from the pack, revealing a single digit. They can place the card in any empty box, either one of their own or one of their opponents. The object is to finish up with the highest total. Say a player turns over a "7"; he or she may decide to put this in the hundreds box for one of their own numbers. But if a "2" is turned over this might be put in a hundreds box of one of their opponents.

When all the boxes are full, each player finds the total of their two numbers (using a calculator) to determine who has the highest score. We find the game works well if the children play ten rounds, writing down their scores after each round and then using their calculators at the end to add up their overall scores. Shuffle the cards between each round.

The game is very popular with children and really helps to focus their attention on the meaning of the digits. They quickly learn that the hundreds are the most significant digits in a three-digit number. Comparing scores at the end of each round and at the end of the game is, of course, an exercise in ordering.

Variations

A fitting extension of the game is based on subtraction rather than addition. Give each player a strip of cardstock with "one" already written in the first of four boxes (see Figure 4.5(b)). This ensures that the first number is larger than the second. In the subtraction version, the children learn that they can help themselves by putting a small digit in the hundreds box of their own second number, or they can mess up their opponent by putting a large digit in the hundreds box of his or her second number.

The game can also be simplified to two-digit numbers or extended to four or more digits. Some students may benefit from trying versions of the game with multiplication; for example, the boxes could be laid out for a two-digit number multiplied by a one-digit number.

Activity 4.8 Say, Press, Check, Write

Materials

A calculator with a constant addition and subtraction facility (most simple school calculators have this); various worksheets with headings set out as in this example:

Targets 18 to 21: working with one place.

SAY, PRESS, CHECK, WRITE

SUBTRACT 1	ADD 2	SUBTRACT 100	ADD 20
404	184	901	150

Method

Children work in pairs to complete the worksheet by writing nine more numbers in each column. For example, in the column headed SUBTRACT 100, they would write: 801, 701, 601, 501, 401, 301, 201, 101 and 1. The procedure is as follows.

The first child, X, enters the number at the top of the column on the calculator, followed by the instruction above it (e.g., "901 – 100"). The second child, Y, says what the answer will be. X then presses the equals key and checks whether this is correct. Then Y writes the correct answer in the column (801). X then says what the next number will be, Y presses the equals key and checks the answer. X writes the correct answer in the column (701). This process continues until the column is complete. Using a calculator with a constant addition and subtraction facility means that only the equals key has to be pressed each time once the initial "–100" has been entered.

Clearly the worksheets can be sequenced to make the tasks gradually more and more difficult, first of all focusing on adding and subtracting 1, then 2, then 10, 20, 100, and 200. Grading of the worksheets should take into account the particular examples highlighted in Targets 18 to 21 (e.g. adding 20 when the tens digit is 8 or 9).

Activity 4.9 What's on the Card?

Materials

A calculator and two packs of cards:
- Pack C: 30 cards, five each with +1, +10, +100, –1, –10, –100 written on one side
- Pack D: 30 cards, five each with +2, +20, +200, –2, –20, –200 written on one side

Targets 18 to 21: concentrating on one place using mental arithmetic.

Method

Depending on the level of difficulty required, the game can be played with either Pack C or Pack D or both packs shuffled together. Player X (or the teacher) chooses a three-digit number between 200 and 800, for example 459. This is written down clearly for both players to see and entered on the calculator. Player X then looks at a card without player Y seeing it, carries out the instruction written on it, and then hands the calculator to Y who has to say what is written on the card. For example, if the calculator is displaying 461, Y should deduce that the card said "+2." If Y is correct and can also get the original number back on display, by applying the inverse operation (e.g. "−2"), he or she wins the card. Otherwise the card goes back in the pack. It is then Y's turn to look at a card and perform the stated operation, and X must deduce what is on the card. The game proceeds until all the cards are won. The winner is the player with the most cards.

Activity 4.10 Grids

Materials
Copies of grids like the one shown in Figure 4.6(a).

> Targets
> 18 to 20: mastering one place using mental arithmetic.

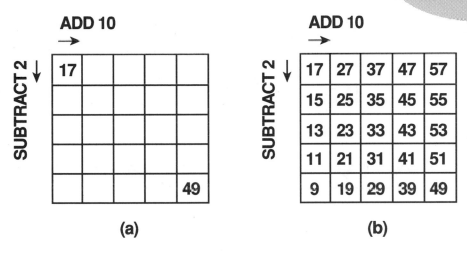

FIGURE 4.6 *Grids (for Activity 4.10)*

Method
The instructions for moving across or moving down the grid can be any combination of ADD 1, SUBTRACT 1, ADD 10, SUBTRACT 10, ADD 100, SUBTRACT 100, ADD 2, SUBTRACT 2, ADD 20, SUBTRACT 20, ADD 200, SUBTRACT 200. A starting number is written in the top left corner and a finishing number in the bottom right corner. Choose these numbers with care. For example, with the instructions ADD 10 and SUBTRACT 2, a starting number of 17 must have a finishing number of 49 (17 + 10 + 10 + 10 + 10 − 2 − 2 − 2 − 2). Writing in the finishing number provides both a check and a target for the students. With low achievers, avoid grids which produce negative numbers. In later years, negative numbers could be attempted for some enrichment, a challenge, or as a target in another unit.

Children work individually to complete these grids, ensuring that they obey the given instruction for all movements left to right along the rows or down the columns. Figure 4.6(b) shows the completed version of the grid given in Figure 4.6(a).

We find it useful to keep a supply of blank grids on which we can quickly write appropriate instructions and numbers. These are given to individual children in quiet moments when other tasks are completed. They are always very popular.

Activity 4.11 Between the Pointers

Materials

A number line, labeled in hundreds and subdivided into tens (see Figure 4.7); three colored pointers (perhaps two red and one blue); and Pack A of cards.

Method

Initially, choose a child who is fairly confident with the number line to act as umpire for this game. For each round, the umpire places the two red pointers on two marks on the number line. In turn, each player turns over three cards from the pack to reveal three digits, then tries to arrange the cards to make a three-digit number which lies between the two numbers indicated by the red pointers. The player then places the blue pointer to show approximately where their number is. If the player gets a number between the red pointers, he or she wins a point, and a second point for positioning it correctly.

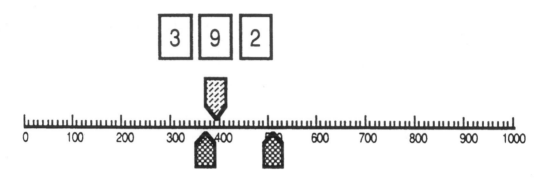

FIGURE 4.7 *Between the pointers (for Activity 4.11)*

In Figure 4.7, the umpire has placed the red pointers at 370 and 510. A player has turned over 2, 3 and 9, rearranged these to form 392 and positioned the blue pointer at about the right point on the number line.

A useful way of introducing the game to the students is to use the overhead projector and number lines and pointers on transparencies. Groups of students could work together using the information on the overhead. Circulate to check the groups of students playing the game together.

Variation

Students can play a simpler version with two-digit numbers and a number line marked in tens and subdivided into units. To make this suitable for dollar notation (Targets 30 and 31), use a modified number line in dollars and have students work with money amounts.

Activity 4.12 Win Some, Lose Some

Materials

Pack A; a supply of pennies, dimes, and one-dollar coins or bills; base-ten blocks; a calculator; and pack E of homemade cards (25 cards, ten with the symbol "+," and five each with the symbols: "–," "x," "=."

Targets
22 and 24
(23 and 25): combining
and taking away
with exchanges.

Method

Each player starts with a float of five one-dollar coins or bills. The first player to achieve 20 is the winner. The first player turns over cards from Pack A and Pack E alternately, laying them out in a row on the table, until an "equals" sign appears. For example, a player might turn up the following sequence:

3 + 8 x 5 – 0 + 2 =

The sequence of calculations displayed must then be worked out, either mentally or using a calculator, to determine the player's winnings. In the example above (working sequentially and not according to the mathematical order of operations), the calculator gives the result "57" and the player is paid five tens and seven ones by the banker. A player must always exchange ten ones for a ten and ten tens for a hundred: failure to do this, if spotted by an opponent, results in a turn being missed.

If a negative answer results, the player has to pay the bank rather than collect. In this case, note that the bank does not give change. However, it will exchange one ten for ten ones or one hundred for ten tens if asked to do so.

If, for example, a player turns up "8" and then a "=" immediately, the turn is complete and that player simply wins 8 cents.

Players get very excited when they produce a long string of cards before an equals sign appears. Of course, the cards are merely a device to generate numbers at random, but there is a considerable pay-off in terms of incidental learning from the game. Children quickly recognize the significance of multiplying by a large digit; they soon start groaning when they get a subtraction sign; they can discover what happens when you multiply by zero; and they get some surprising insights into negative numbers. But the main purpose of the game is to give practice in the process of exchange in addition and subtraction.

Variations

(i) Play the same game with base-ten blocks to focus on Targets 23 and 25.

(ii) To generate three-digit answers more frequently, allow players to turn over two cards from Pack A once in each turn (as long as they don't hit the = sign, which ends their turn). A shrewd player might wait for a multiplication sign to appear before taking this option, for example, scoring 384 with:

3 + 5 x 48 =

Note: This sequential approach does not conform to the conventional order of operations. For example, multiplication should be done before addition. Using such a convention, "4 + 5 x 2" would equal 14 (i.e., "4 + 10"), since the multiplication would be done first. Scientific calculators (those that use what is called an algebraic operating system) use these conventions and give the answer "14" if the calculation "4 + 5 x 2 =" is keyed in. However, the simple calculators normally used by elementary school children do not use these conventions. They simply perform the calculations in the order in which they are entered. So, keying in "4 + 5 x 2 =" on a regular calculator produces the answer "18" (i.e. 9 x 2), since the addition, entered first, is done first.

We might be accused of creating a situation in which students will experience the truths of mathematics as unstable. We believe that the conventions of order of operations are only important when students move on to manipulating algebraic expressions. In practical arithmetic calculations, the context always determines the order in which the operations should be performed. In our view, it is quite inappropriate to raise the question of these conventions with our low-achieving students in this age range. We are therefore quite happy to ignore the conventions in Activity 4.12 and to follow the logic of the simple calculator which takes the sequence of operations in the order they appear.

Activity 4.13 Spend Ten Dollars

Materials
Pack A and Pack B (or some other means of generating two-digit numbers) and a supply of pennies, dimes, and one-dollar coins or bills.

Target 24 (25): taking away with exchange.

Method
This is simply the reverse of the game described in Activity 4.3. Players start with ten dollars and race to be the first to spend all their money. Once again, the bank does not give change, but will exchange ten ones for a ten or ten tens for a hundred, if requested. This ensures that the place-value target is addressed.

Variation
Play the same game with base-ten blocks, starting with a thousand block, to focus on Target 25.

Activity 4.14 What's Your Total?
This individual or small group activity is led by the teacher, possibly with the assistance of a "mail carrier." This activity has the added advantage of making connections with cheques, bills (real-life expenses), and purchasing power.

Targets 5 and 6 (22 to 25): connections among language, symbols, and concrete materials.

Materials
Calculators, one per student or at least one per group and two sets of envelopes, one with cheques and one with bills. Duplicate the cheques and bills on different colors of paper and place them in different kinds of envelopes to make the difference clear to students. The amounts of the cheques and bills should be written in various forms: in dollar notation, in words, as total number of cents. The students must translate each amount to a numeral that can be entered on the calculator. To ensure that negative balances do not result, deliver more cheques than bills and make the bills smaller amounts than the cheques.

Method
Students receive a "mail delivery" from the teacher or designated mail carrier. They open the envelope, record the amount in the appropriate column, and enter it on the

calculator. Students then receive another mail delivery and incorporate the new amount, either a cheque or a bill, into the balance making the correct entries. The object of the game is to keep track of the correct amount and figure out what the balance or total is.

Variations

After the deliveries, students can spend their money, trying to have less than one dollar remaining. Students can invent the merchandise they want to buy or they can work from a teacher-prepared list or a commercial catalogue.

Activity 4.15 Money Notation Practice

Targets 26 to 29: translating calculator answers into money notation.

Materials

Coins, calculator, worksheets.

Method

Using both coins and the calculator, children work through a set of examples focusing on interpreting calculator displays with just one digit after the decimal point, such as:
1. How much does it cost for a book at $3.25 and a pen at $1.45? (Use +.)
2. Share $19.20 among 3 people. How much does each get? (Use ÷.)
3. How much will you pay for 5 burgers at $1.22 each? (Use x.)
4. How much change will you get from a $5.00 bill if you spend $3.70? (Use −)

In the first question, for example, the students would lay out the two sums of money in coins and establish that the total is $4.70. But when they enter "3.25 + 1.45 =" on the calculator, they get the result "4.7."

Further examples, using division only, focus on the problem of interpreting calculator displays with more than two digits after the decimal point:
5. Share $4.25 among 3 people. How much does each get? (Use ÷)

Here the students would put out $4.25 in coins, and, exchanging where necessary, divide this into three piles of $1.41, with 2 cents left over. Then they would enter "4.25 ÷ 3 =" on the calculator to get the result 1.4166666. You may have to explain what is going on: the calculator tries to share out the 2 cents and gives each person some little bits of pennies. We can just give the result as "1.41 and a little bit" or a "remainder." Usually, of course, "1.41" would do, since the little bits are not big enough to concern us.

Activity 4.16 Is the Price Right?

This activity has the added advantage of a direct real-life application.

Targets 30 and 31: ordering dollar amounts.

Materials

Commercial sale flyer or a sheet with items and corresponding prices, prepared by the teacher or students.

Method

After presenting the flyers and allowing some time for unstructured examination, ask students to find the most and/or least expensive items on the sheet or flyer. If there are many items, ask them to find the most or least expensive of a particular kind of item, such as radios, toys, or cars. Challenge the students to think critically by asking if those items seem to be good deals or not. Ask students which items are in the middle and arrange them in order. Students can imagine that they are buying a gift for a friend or relative and have a budget with both upper and lower limits. Which items fall within their limits? Which item would they actually purchase? Why?

More activities

To focus further on the targets for money notation, some of the activities suggested above can be adapted. Some of these suggestions are incorporated in the unit for teaching money (see Chapter 8).

For example: the games described in Activities 4.2, 4.3, 4.12, and 4.13 could all include a recording element, each player being required to keep a written record, using dollar notation, of their gains (or losses) and remaining balance.

- In Activity 4.7, the boxes could be set out with a $ sign and a decimal point

$$ \$\ .\ \square\ \square\ +\$\ \square\ .\ \square\ \square $$

- In Activity 4.8, the "say, press, check, write" sequences could include instructions to add or subtract 1 cents, 10 cent, 1 dollar, 2 cents, 20 cents, or 2 dollars, and the results written down in dollar notation. For example:

SUBTRACT 1 cent	ADD 2 cents	SUBTRACT 1 dollar	ADD 20 cents
4.04	1.84	9.01	1.50

Key teaching points

- Use familiar and meaningful models of the place-value system such as money, base-ten blocks, and possibly metric measures.
- Show connections among words, mathematical symbols, concrete representations, and real-life situations.
- Allow time for students to think about what the number system means; help them to verbalize their new understandings.

QUESTIONS FOR DISCUSSION WITH COLLEAGUES

1. In your experience, what are some of the problems children have when handling zero? Why does zero cause so many difficulties? What has worked for you and your students?

2. Is the set of targets an adequate description of what it means to understand place value? Are these targets realistic for low achievers up to the age of 12? How do they compare with the local curriculum targets for children of that age?

3. How can the activities of this chapter be integrated with real-life experiences of the place-value system? How have you noticed progress in your students' understanding of place value and their ability to manage real-life situations involving place value?

4. What improvements or modifications can you make to the activities in this chapter that might increase the learning opportunities for your particular students?

5 Measurement ....

An overview of measurement

Learning to cope with the measurements we encounter in everyday life is an essential component of numeracy. A few years ago Derek observed a group of 11- and 12-year-olds working on the topic of length. They were struggling with questions like this in their textbook:

> Should we help our students become experts at measurement or experts at doing textbook problems about measurement (or both)?

$$1 \text{ m } 55 \text{ cm}$$
$$+ 2 \text{ m } 48 \text{ cm}$$

At the same time, the school buildings were undergoing some major renovations. Carpenters were taking down interior walls and building closets and bookcases for a library. These men were clearly experts at linear measurement, using tape-measures, rulers, levels, and set squares with great accuracy and confidence. Derek was struck by the enormous gulf between the purposeless tasks the students were doing and the purposeful applications of the concepts of length demonstrated by the carpenters.

Out of interest, Derek asked one of the workers to try some of the questions in the students' textbook. This expert at measurement struggled as much as some of the students — a helpful lesson in demonstrating the difference between knowing math out of context and using math in real life.

Five aspects of measurement are considered suitable for work with low achievers: length and distance, mass, capacity and liquid volume, time, and temperature. For each aspect of measurement, we designed a set of targets to include:

- knowledge of terms, facts, definitions, and principles;
- mastery of techniques and manipulative skills;
- understanding of concepts, procedures, and principles; and
- application of knowledge, skills, and understanding.

Targets for measurment emphasize understanding as much as skills and knowledge. Even where we have deliberately limited the targets to what might be realistic for low achievers, each set of targets should advance the students far enough that they are able to use the skills and concepts of measurement in some purposeful applications. The activities found in the second part of the chapter include examples of such purposeful applications. Students should be able to "understand the attributes of length, capacity, weight, area, volume, time, temperature, and angle; make and use estimates of measurement; make and use measurements in problem and every-day situations; apply estimation in working with… measurement; estimate, make, and use measurements to describe and compare phenomena" (NCTM, 1989, pp. 51, 36, 116).

Understanding how time is measured and recorded is clearly necessary for organizing one's life: for catching buses, planes, and trains, and for following any sort of timetable. This should be a major focus of our work, especially because of the complications of the non-decimal system of measuring and recording time. Length and distance are the easiest measuring concepts for children to grasp, and provide a useful and accessible experience of the basic principles of measurement. Mass is encountered in shopping and general conversations, as are capacity and liquid volume. A favorite topic of conversation is the weather, and with that the temperature.

We have excluded area, solid volume, and angle. Area and volume, apart from some preliminary experiences such as filling spaces with tiles and building solids with cubes, are not often used and children find the concepts difficult to handle. Angles would be better placed in a unit on geometry which included lines, planes, circles, and intersections. Although some experiences with these concepts are appropriate for our students, we decided not to present them here. Instead, we concentrate on developing confidence in the five aspects of measurement listed above.

Competence and confidence in measurement is essential for making sense of and living in our world.

Developing understanding and skills in measurement

Comparison and ordering

The first stage of learning to measure anything is to understand how to compare two things directly and to determine which is the greater or lesser according to the attribute in question. To make these comparisons, the students need to use the language of comparison. For example, we might place two students side by side and determine which is taller and which shorter; or we might place two objects in the pans of a balance and determine which is heavier and which lighter. We might pour water from one container into another and decide which holds more and which holds less, or two students might undertake a task and discover who takes longer and who takes a shorter time to complete it.

> One effective way to teach measurement concepts is to compare items with respect to the attribute in question.

From direct comparison of two things, the students should then learn to order a set of three or more things according to the attribute being measured. Again this is done by direct comparison without any units being involved.

Conservation

When developing an understanding of length, mass, and liquid volume, the student should grasp the principle of conservation. This means that the quantity is unchanged, even when the object being measured is subjected to certain transformations. For example, the length of an object is unchanged when the object is moved to a new position or curled up in some way, the mass of a lump of modeling clay is unchanged when it is broken up into a number of smaller pieces, and the volume of water in a container is unchanged when it is poured into a different shaped container.

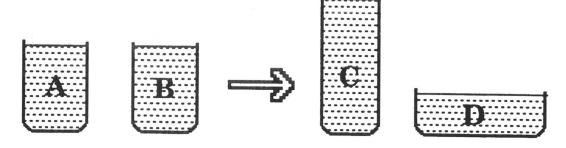

FIGURE 5.1 *Conservation of liquid volume*

Recognizing the students' grasp of these ideas is, however, difficult. Their response to some questions might indicate that they have not grasped the principle, whereas their response to other questions or their behavior in other situations might indicate that they have. For example, some 10-year-olds in a mathematics class failed one of the standard tests of conservation of volume. When the water in containers A and B, shown in Figure

5.1, was poured into containers C and D respectively, the students responded that C had more water in it than D. The orthodox interpretation of this response is that the students are focusing on the height of the water rather than the volume, although there are other plausible explanations.

When some students came in sweaty and thirsty from recess, Derek engaged two students in a role play. He filled a container with some orange juice and poured this into a glass tumbler. Then he did the same, this time pouring it into a second, different shaped tumbler. He passed the drinks out and the students who had previously failed the conservation test were now quite certain that what he had done was fair. It was clear that they recognized that the two children had received the same amount of juice.

When working on the targets related to conservation, determine whether or not the principles have been grasped by observing the student's behavior or responses in situations that have some meaning for them.

Nonstandard units

Students should begin to measure each attribute using nonstandard units such as hand spans for length, pebbles for mass, and paper cups for capacity. By using familiar items, they gain experience with the idea of measuring in units and develop a clearer idea of what it is that is being measured. Often the sizes of these nonstandard units are more appropriate for measuring the objects in the student's environment than standard units are.

> The use of nonstandard units, estimation, and reference items focuses attention on the concepts of measurement and away from the distracting finer points of technical precision.

Estimation

Each set of targets for measurement includes a reference to the ability to estimate a quantity, such as the length or mass of an object, the capacity of a container, or the length of a time interval. Each of these targets specifies what we would judge, from our experience, to be a reasonable level of accuracy to expect from low-achieving students of this age group.

We have found that experiences aimed at developing the ability to make reasonable estimates for measurements are some of the most successful and effective ways of increasing our students' confidence with each aspect of measurement. Some suggestions for such experiences are given toward the end of the chapter.

Reference items

To help students make these estimates and therefore to build their confidence with measurement, we find it helpful to give them some reference items. These are simply familiar objects for which they can memorize a measurement and then use this for reference in comparisons with other objects. For example, Derek found that the students who made the best progress in capacity measurements were those who knew that a can of pop was 350 mL and who used this frequently as a reference item.

Approximation

Even at this early stage, introduce students to the idea that measurement is always approximate. We can only ever measure something to the nearest unit. The key language to be developed here is "to the nearest" and "between...and...." For example students might record the length of a corridor as being "nearly 25 steps" or "between 24 and 25 steps." These language structures also apply to other aspects of measurement.

> This is a key understanding: All measurement is approximate. The degree of precision is a decision of the person measuring makes, depending on the demands of the situation.

Standard units

For each aspect of measurement, we must decide which standard units are appropriate for our students to use. Apart from measuring time, where students must learn to use seconds, minutes, hours, days, weeks, months, and years, we have found it best to limit the number of different units we introduce, guided by the units most frequently used in everyday situations, such as shopping and cooking. In the targets below, we refer only to the following units: centimeter and meter for length (or inch, foot, and yard), gram and kilogram for mass (ounce and pound), and milliliter and liter for capacity and liquid volume (or cup, pint, and gallon).

Metric and imperial units

Throughout this book we have used examples which have either metric or imperial units. This is an attempt to be more inclusive when writing for both Canadian and American audiences. Since the structure of the examples is the important feature we want to stress, the units could be switched from metric to imperial or vice versa without losing the key teaching points. Therefore, when necessary, we ask our readers to mentally substitute appropriate units into illustrative examples and activities. At the same time, we cannot ignore the fact that many imperial units have survived attempts to completely metricate Canada. But difficult decisions are involved here. We aim for relevant targets, but we must also be realistic about what can be achieved. We cannot really expect our low achievers to cope with all the units that they might hear people using:

"Just a couple of inches wide."

"He's nearly six feet tall."

"The ball is on the 10-yard line."

"I weigh 162 pounds."

"Use three cups of flour for the pancakes."

"My car does about 35 miles to the gallon."

Canadian teachers may well question our limited reference to imperial units. Because of their practical experience outside of school, many students can cope confidently with many imperial measures used in everyday activities. Later in life, some will be involved in construction businesses that still use feet, inches, and pounds. We advise teachers to be judicious when introducing a large number of units.

Developing decimal notation

Restricting the number of units for measuring provides our low achievers with a sound introduction to decimal notation in practical contexts. They should first have mastered the dollar notation for money, such as $1.75 as an alternative way of writing 175¢, as outlined in place-value targets 26 to 31 in Chapter 4. An exact parallel can then be drawn when measuring in centimeters: a length of 175 cm can also be written as 1.75 m. Stress that both work the same way, because there are 100 cents in a dollar and 100 centimeters in a meter. With low achievers we stick to the same conventions for recording length as we use for money. When writing a length (such as 150 cm) in meters, we use two digits after the decimal point: i.e., 1.50 m rather than 1.5 m. The parallel with 150¢ = $1.50 is very helpful and should be reinforced as much as possible.

Use of the metric system provides reinforcement of decimal notation.

When measuring mass, we have 1000 grams in a kilogram, so now we get three digits after the decimal point. A mass of 1550 g can also be written as 1.550 kg. Low-achieving students seem to get the idea that this is just the same as dollars and cents, but with three digits rather than two because of the 1000 g in a kilogram. It is neither necessary nor realistic to explain that the first digit after the decimal point represents tenths of a kilogram, the second hundredths of a kilogram, and the third thousandths of a kilogram. We simply build on and extend the everyday experience of handling money notation. Then, of course, milliliters and liters behave in just the same way as grams and kilograms: 1550 mL = 1.550 liters.

Consequently, the students have two practical experiences of handling numbers with two digits after the decimal point (money and length) and two with three digits after the decimal point (mass and capacity). We feel this is sufficient competence for low-achieving students up to the age of 12 years, and a sound basis for future development of work with decimal fractions.

Measuring devices

When developing skills of measuring we have to decide which measuring devices students should learn to use and in which order (see Figure 5.2). For example, we recommend that they use just kilogram, 100-gram, 10-gram and 1-gram masses on balances. This experience provides a useful reinforcement of place-value concepts: something that weighs 345 grams, for example, is balanced by 3 hundreds, 4 tens and 5 units. Students who use the American system can use 1 lb., 8 oz., 4 oz., and 1 oz. weights to parallel the common fraction system of 1 lb., 1/2 lb., 1/4 lb., and 1/16 lb.

Reduce complexity to allow students to become proficient with a narrower range of devices.

Attribute to be Measured	Units	Measuring Devices
Length	1 km 1 m, 1 cm	30 cm ruler, metre stick tape measure
Mass (weight)	1 kg, 100 g, 10 g, 1 g 1 lb.	double pan balance
Capacity and Liquid Volume	1 L, 1 mL 1 cup, 1 ounce	graduated containers of all kinds
Time	1 hr, 1 min, 1 sec 1 yr, 1 mth, 1 day 1 week	12 hr digital clocks analog clocks calendars
Temperature	1°C (1°F)	thermometers

Figure 5.2 *Measuring devices*

Learning targets for length and distance

Units for length and distance

In Canada, we think that we can dispense with inches, feet, and yards in the classroom in our work with low achievers and concentrate on meters and centimeters, at least initially.

We have excluded millimeters (1000 mm = 1 m), partly because they are small and hard to work with and partly because of the complications involved in handling the extra relationships involved, such as 135 mm = 13.5 cm = 0.135 m. However, when the students are confident with centimeters and meters, it may be useful to introduce millimeters toward the end of the 8–12 age range if a greater degree of accuracy is required in practical tasks, especially since millimeters are used extensively in many trades and scientific work. Teachers in the United States will need to modify the targets by adapting the units for their own situations.

Reference items for length

To help our students develop a sense of the size of the units we use for measuring length, some useful reference items are:

(a) a child's finger is about 1 cm (1/4 in.) wide;

(b) the students' rulers are 30 cm (12 in. or 1 ft.) long;

(c) a meter stick, used for pointing, is 100 cm (yard stick is 36 in.) long;

(d) the classroom door is about 200 cm or 2 m (2 1/4 yds.) high.

> You may be wise to observe your students or even interview them to find out which items of length might make the best reference items.

When the topic of length is being taught or used in other contexts, refer to these facts repeatedly for comparison with other objects in the classroom. Children should use them often enough to memorize them. For measuring longer distances, athletic track events may provide relevant reference items. Important language concepts throughout this topic are the words used for comparison: longer, shorter, taller, higher, lower, wider, narrower, farther, nearer.

Applications

Some of the targets address the category of application, such as the use of scale drawings. This is potentially a difficult aspect of mathematics, but, provided a one-to-one scale is employed, low-achieving 12-year-old students can use this idea to tackle some interesting and purposeful problems. Plan in advance the size of grid on the squared paper used for the students' scale drawings, in order that, for example, one meter measured can be represented by one unit on the scale drawing.

The concepts, skills, and knowledge of length measurement can also be applied to various construction tasks. An important associated skill is the use of a set square for drawing right angles.

Realistic and relevant targets for length and distance

See Activities 5.1, 5.10, and 5.11.

Students will have a basic competence in handling the concepts of length and distance if they are able:

1. To order a set of two or three objects by length, height, or width, using the language "longer than," "taller than," "shorter than," "wider than," and "narrower than" correctly to describe the ordering. (No units at this stage: comparisons are made directly by placing objects side by side.)

2. To choose and use an appropriate nonstandard unit of length (e.g., digit, span, or cubit) to measure the length of an object.

3. To state the results of Target 2 using the language "is about . . . units" and "is between . . . and . . . units" (for example, "the length of the desk is about 8 spans" or "the length of the desk is between 8 and 9 spans").

4. To measure and compare distances, using paces and the language "farther than" and "nearer than" (for example, it is 90 paces to the front entrance and 55 paces to the hall; the front entrance is farther away than the hall).

5. To recognize that the length of a given object is unchanged when it is moved to a new position (conservation of length).

6. To measure the length of a room, a corridor, or a distance in the playground in meters, using a meter stick or a trundle wheel.

7. To measure the linear dimensions of a familiar (classroom) object to the nearest centimeter, using a 30-cm ruler, a meter ruler, or a tape measure.

8. To recall that 1 meter is 100 cm.

9. To draw a line or measure out a distance of a given length in centimeters or meters, using appropriate measuring devices.

10. To measure and compare the lengths, widths, or heights of two objects and, using a calculator if necessary, to formulate statements using the appropriate language of comparison (for example, if person X is 125 cm tall, and person Y is 143 cm tall, to state that person X is 18 cm shorter than person Y).

11. To recall the lengths of some specific objects or distances used as reference items, including a 30-cm ruler and a meter stick.

12. To estimate by eye the length of an object in centimeters, up to 200 cm, to within 25% either way (for example, given a length of 80 cm, any estimate between 60 cm and 100 cm would be acceptable).
13. To recall approximately how far it is in kilometers to significant places from their home (for example, how far to school or how far to Ottawa or Saskatoon).
14. To translate correctly between centimeters and meters (for example, 185 cm = 1.85 m).
15. To use a simple one-to-one scale to make scale drawings.
16. To follow instructions for construction tasks involving measurements in centimeters, including the use of a set square for making right angles.

Learning targets for weight

Weight and Mass

Strictly speaking, we should not say that the weight of an apple is 300 grams, but that the mass of the apple is 300 grams, or that the apple weighs the same as 300 grams. This is because grams (kilograms, pounds etc.) are actually units of mass. Technically the weight of an object is the force of gravity acting on a given mass, and should therefore be measured in the units of force, such as newtons. (See Haylock and Cockburn (1997) for a fuller discussion of this issue.) We have not maintained the distinction between weight and mass simply because in practice most people talk about weight when they actually mean mass. To be pedantic about the language here will unnecessarily confuse students who often have special deficiencies in language anyway, and we must therefore just concede to the colloquial usage. In the rest of this book, we use the common expression "weight" when we are referring to "mass." C'est la vie!

Units for weight

Imperial units continue to cause confusion. In Canada, prepackaged produce is sold in both metric and imperial units, but most fruit and vegetables from a farmers' market stall are sold by the pound. It is common to buy, for example, 1/4 pound of ham from the supermarket delicatessen counter, but the prepackaged sliced meats are in metric packages. Although recipes in most Canadian cookbooks give the amounts of ingredients in grams and mL, many give them in cup measures as well. We cannot ignore in the classroom the student's experience of weight outside of it, so we must make some limited recognition of these continuing uses of imperial units. It is particularly important for low-achieving students to build on their day-to-day experiences and to relate what we do in mathematics lessons to the real world. Therefore, some concessions to the real-world use of imperial units are necessary. We have therefore included some targets related to pounds.

Reference items for weight

To help our students develop a sense of the size of the units we use for measuring weight, the following reference items may be useful (use convenient reference items for your local area).
(a) an individual bag of potato chips weighs 30 grams;
(b) a standard size tin of baked beans weighs about 500 grams (including the tin);
(c) a liter of water weighs a kilogram (1000 grams).

Make items such as these available for comparison in the classroom when teaching the topic of weight. Children should also memorize their own weight.

Realistic and relevant learning targets for weight

Students will have a basic competence in handling the concepts of weight in practical situations if they are able:

1. To order a set of two or three objects by weight using a simple balance, and to use the language "is heavier than" and "is lighter than" correctly to describe the ordering. (No units at this stage: comparisons are made directly by balancing one object against another.)

> Important aspects of language are the words used for comparison: "heavier than" and "lighter than."

2. To choose and use an appropriate nonstandard unit of weight and a simple balance to weigh an object.

3. To state the results of Target 2 using the language "weighs about the same as" and "weighs between... and ..." (for example, "the book weighs about the same as 9 pebbles" or "the book weighs between 9 and 10 pebbles").

> See Activities 5.1, 5.2, and 5.3.

4. To recognize that the weight of a given object is unchanged when its shape is transformed or when it is reassembled in some way (conservation of weight).

5. To use a simple balance and 1-gram, 10-gram, 100-gram and 1-kilogram weights to measure the weight of an object.

6. To recall that 1 kilogram is 1000 g, that half a kilogram is 500 g, and that a quarter of a kilogram is 250 g. (If students are unfamiliar with fractions, use the words for half and quarter, not the symbols. See Chapter 6 for a fuller treatment of the language of fractions.)

7. Use a spring-type weighing device to weigh an object (for example, to use kitchen scales to determine that a book weighs 350 g).

8. To follow the instructions for the preparation of a meal (or science experiment) by measuring out a given weight of some substance in grams or ounces using a balance-type or a spring-type weighing device (for example, to measure out 250 g of fruit for a portion of a meal).

9. To measure and compare the weights of two objects and, using a calculator if necessary, to formulate statements using "is . . . heavier than" or "is . . . lighter than" (for example, if object X is found to weigh 250 g and object Y to weigh 750 g, to state that object X is 500 g lighter than object Y).

10. To recall the mass in grams of some reference items, including a liter of water (1000 g). (See comments above regarding reference items.)

11. To estimate, by holding in the hand, the mass of an object in grams up to 1000 g but not less than 25 g, to within 40% either way (for example, given a container holding 100 g of something, any estimate between 60 g and 140 g would be acceptable).

12. To determine, by holding in the hand, whether a given object has a weight which is less than, about equal to, or more than (a) a kilogram, (b) 100 g, (c) a pound, and (d) half a pound. (Use fairly obvious cases: for example, a book might be recognized as weighing less than a kilogram but more than 100 g.)

13. To translate correctly between grams and kilograms (for example, 750 g = 0.750 kg).
14. To use conversion charts between imperial and metric units which occur in cooking. (This might involve, for example, conversion between mL and cups).

Learning targets for capacity and liquid volume

Units for capacity and liquid volume

Capacity refers to the volume of a liquid that can be held by a container. In the metric system, liquid volume and capacities are both measured in liters or milliliters (1 liter = 1000 mL). The ease of using the decimal measurements is an advantage of the metric system over the imperial system which uses ounces and cups. Cubic centimeters and cubic meters, also units for measuring volume, are, by convention, reserved for volumes of solids.

Most items sold by volume in supermarkets are measured in liters or milliliters (mL). To avoid the confusion caused by using different units such as deciliters and centiliters, use just milliliters and liters. Once liter and milliliter are firmly in their minds, our students might be able to deal with the other units.

Fluid cups occur only in recipes; nothing (in Canada) is sold in fluid ounces, although some containers have the fluid ounce equivalent on the label. Most recipes in Canadian cookbooks that give liquid volumes in cups also give them in milliliters, so we suggest that you exclude fluid cups from their experience in school. Also in Canada, gasoline is sold in liters even though efficiency is commonly referred to as miles per gallon (rather than the technically correct but unpopular liters per 100 km) but we also exclude any reference to gallons.

Reference Items for capacity and liquid volume

Helpful reference items for developing the students' sense of the size of the metric units for capacity and liquid volume might be the following (use items commonly found in your area).
(a) a standard can of pop, 350 mL;
(b) a plastic pop bottle, 750 mL;
(c) a one-liter carton of milk or juice.

Children should memorize the capacities of these reference containers. Keep them available in the classroom and refer to them repeatedly, comparing them with other containers. The key language for comparison here is "holds more than" and "holds less than."

Realistic and relevant targets for capacity and liquid volume

Students will have a basic competence in handling the concepts of capacity and liquid volume in practical situations if they are able:

See Activities 5.1 and 5.9.

1. To order the capacities of two or three containers by pouring liquid from one to another.
2. To choose an appropriate nonstandard unit (teaspoon, paper cup, etc.) to measure and compare the capacities of two given containers.
3. To recognize that a given volume of water is unchanged when poured from one container to another (conservation of volume).

4. To recognize that the shape of the container is not a determining property of capacity.

5. To use a liter container to measure the approximate capacity of a larger container (for example, to measure the capacity of a bucket by filling it with liters of water).

6. To use a calibrated measuring cup to measure the capacity of a container in mL.

7. To follow the instructions in a recipe (or a science experiment) to measure out a given quantity of liquid in mL (for example, to measure 250 mL of milk for a pancake recipe).

8. To recall that 1 liter is 1000 mL, that a half liter is 500 mL, and that a quarter liter is 250 mL.

9. To measure and compare the capacities of two containers and, using a calculator if necessary, to formulate statements using "holds ... more than" or "holds ... less than" (for example, if container A is found to hold 250 mL and container B to hold 750 mL, to state that container A holds 500 mL less than B).

10. To recall the capacity in mL of a pop can (350 mL, about 1/3 of a liter), a plastic pop bottle (750 mL) and a one-liter milk or juice carton (1000 mL).

11. To estimate an amount of liquid in a container in mL, up to 1000 mL, to within 40% either way (for example, given a container holding 100 mL, any estimate between 60 mL and 140 mL would be acceptable).

12. To determine, by eye, whether the capacity of a given container is less than, about equal to, or more than a liter.

13. To translate correctly between milliliters and liters (for example, 750 mL = 0.750 L).

Learning targets for time

Time intervals and recorded time

We develop two aspects of time, both very important components of numeracy and both necessary for coping confidently with the demands of everyday life. First is the notion of a time interval — the length of time which passes between two instants or the amount of time that an event or activity takes. For example, we might say that the mathematics lesson lasts for one hour. Second is the idea of recorded time: the time at which an event occurs. We might say that the mathematics lesson begins at 9:20 a.m. The idea of recorded time can include days of the week, dates, and years; for example, the mathematics lesson began at 9:20 a.m. on Wednesday, May 3rd, 2000. Children need to learn both how to measure and manipulate time intervals and how to tell and record the time of day.

Poll your class to see what kind of watches and clocks they use at school and at home.

Digital or dial?

A major problem in teaching children to tell the time is that many of your students have digital watches and first learned to tell the time using these. A further complication is that some of these digital watches may use the 24-hour system. Most classroom clocks have a dial, and most math programs seem to concentrate on telling the time from dial clocks first. As teachers, we have to decide how best to build on the children's first-hand experience of telling the time. So, what is the actual situation with regard to children's personal watches? Determine how typical the following data is in your own teaching situation.

In a recent survey of about 1000 children in the 8-12 age range in several British schools, Derek found that only 32% actually wore a watch to school. Of those watches, 45% were dial watches with hands (no digital display), 50% had digital displays only, and 5% had both digital and dial displays. Of the watches with digital displays, 45% could give the time in the 24-hour system (some digital watches give both the 12-hour and the 24-hour time).

As expected, more of the older students wore watches. There was also a marked tendency for more girls than boys to wear dial watches, and more boys than girls to wear digital watches.

It is, of course, easier to read the time from a digital display than from a clock face. The connection between the different forms of stating the time is especially difficult. This, combined with the data about the children's own watches, suggests that we might give more prominence in the early stages to telling the time by digital displays, thus using times in the form "3:45" before learning to read "quarter-to-four" from a conventional dial clock. This reverses the normal order used in many schools for developing the skills of telling the time. We suggest that you display a digital clock on the wall of your class-room as well as a dial clock: this is probably one of the most effective ways of achieving many of the targets for time.

The 24-hour system

This then leaves the question of the 24-hour system. We have decided to omit this, because it seems to cause considerable difficulties in learning. We already have two ways of giving the time, with, for example, "3:40 p.m." and "twenty-to-four in the after-noon." To add "1540" to this is to increase the complications. Few if any students use the 24-hour system on their digital watches. Some occupational groups and institu-tions use the 24-hour system, but our students will have plenty of time to learn it before entering the work force.

Some comments on the time targets

The first group of time targets focuses on measuring time intervals. The students progress from time comparisons, through measuring time intervals with nonstandard units, to measuring and estimating time intervals in seconds. The obvious problem with measuring long time intervals is that it takes a long time! But, through explicit discussion of the events of their lives, students should develop some awareness of what ten minutes, an hour, etc., feel like. The next group of targets focuses on recorded time, using a digital display of the 12-hour system.

When the students have a grasp of time intervals and can also tell the time from a digital display, move them on to calculating time intervals, preferably using practical and realistic problems. We have seen low achievers struggling needlessly with formal calcula-tions of this kind, so we assert that these problems not be set out with one time written above the other in the form of a subtraction algorithm. In this case, informal methods are far superior and are used routinely by most people, including adults.

Learning targets related to telling time from a conventional dial clock include the important ideas of "nearly" and "just after." They also include the ability to translate between the different ways of recording time of day. We do not included the task of drawing the hands on a clock-face to show a given time of day. This is a pointless skill, especially for low achievers.

Targets for recorded time also include the use and understanding of a calendar. Finally, we include three important applications of the knowledge, skills, and concepts of time.

Children will bring a variety of experiences of clocks and watches. Therefore, the sequence for achieving the targets will differ for each student.

Realistic and relevant targets for time

Students will have a basic competence in handling the concepts of time intervals and recorded time in practical situations if they are able:

1. To make sensible statements about which of two familiar events takes a longer or a shorter time. (For example, which takes the shorter time, school assembly or a football game?)

2. To time activities or events using nonstandard units such as a pendulum or a tap dripping.

3. To time activities or events in seconds, using the second counter of a digital watch starting from zero, or a simple stopwatch.

See Activities 5.1, 5.4–5.8, 5.12, and 5.13.

4. To make sensible statements about what they could do in one minute, two minutes, five minutes, ten minutes. (For example, about how many pages of their favorite book could they read in ten minutes?)

5. To estimate a time interval in seconds, by counting, up to a minute, to within 25% either way. (For example, given an interval of 45 seconds, any estimate between 34 seconds and 56 seconds would be acceptable.)

6. To make sensible statements about how long events within their experience take, in minutes up to an hour, and in hours up to a day (for example, that walking to school takes about ten minutes or they spend about six hours in school each day).

7. To state the number of seconds in a minute, the number of minutes in an hour, the number of hours in a day, and the number of days in a week.

8. To state the number of minutes in a quarter of an hour, half an hour, and three-quarters of an hour.

9. To convert a time interval related to their experience (up to 5 hours) from hours and minutes to minutes only, and vice versa. (For example, a regulation hockey game often lasts 2 hours 30 minutes = 150 minutes.)

10. To use correctly the notions of morning, noon, afternoon, evening, night-time, midnight, and the o'clocks, when describing events of their day (for example, to say what they will be doing at six o'clock in the evening).

11. To state what would be displayed on a 12-hour digital watch at significant times of the day (for example, at the start of school, end of school, bed-time).

12. To describe what happens on a 12-hour digital watch display from one minute to the next, from one hour to the next, and in the course of a day. (For example, when the watch shows 3:59, what will it show next? What will it show one hour later?)

13. To distinguish between a.m. and p.m.

14. To reset a 12-hour digital watch or clock to the correct time.

15. To calculate how many minutes must pass from any given time on a 12-hour digital display to the next o'clock. (For example, if the clock now shows 3:48, how many minutes are there until 4 o'clock?)

16. To calculate, by an informal adding-on process, the time interval from one digital time to another. (For example, to find the time for a car trip starting at 3:45 p.m. and arriving at 5:25 p.m., the student could count 15 minutes to 4 p.m., then an hour to 5 p.m., then a further 25 minutes, giving a total of 1 hour 40 minutes. Note especially the problems with events starting before noon and finishing after noon.)

17. To read a conventional dial (analog) clock for o'clocks, half past, quarter past, and quarter to the hour.

18. To describe how the hands of a dial clock behave in one hour, two hours, 12 hours, a day, half an hour, and quarter of an hour.

19. To tell the time to the nearest five minutes from a dial clock or watch, giving the answer in the colloquial form (for example, "twenty to four").

20. To use the expressions "nearly" and "just after" appropriately when reading the time from a dial clock.

21. To reset a dial clock to the correct time (preferable to drawing hands on clock faces!).

22. To translate between times from a dial clock and the digital equivalents in the 12-hour system (for example, to read a time of "half past two in the afternoon" and to convert this to "2:30 p.m.").

23. To order a set of times of the day given in a variety of forms, from earliest to latest (for example, to order: 3:40 p.m., 12 noon, twenty to four in the morning).

24. To recite the names of the days of the week, the months of the year, and the seasons, in order, starting from any day, any month, or any season.

25. To state the number of days in each month and the number of days in a year and in a leap year.

26. To use a calendar to find and record the date, using two common systems (for example, August 24th, 2003, 24/08/03, or whatever system they will usually experience).

27. To use a calendar to find the number of days or weeks from one given date to another.

28. To explain briefly the relationships between the Earth's rotation and a day and the Earth's orbit round the sun and a year.

29. To compile a timetable for an event, given constraints of starting time, finishing time, number of activities, and length of time for each activity.

30. To set automatic timing devices (for example, timers and electric ovens).

31. To program a video recorder to record several television shows.

Learning targets for temperature

In Canada, the Fahrenheit system has been officially banished to antiquity and the Celsius scale is used for weather reports and for such things as label warnings for paint and computer disks. Although oven dials generally read in Fahrenheit, students only need to read the recipe and set the temperature. Therefore, we recommend using Celsius only, at least at first. Students will quickly learn, if they haven't already, that measures of temperature in either scale go up when it is hot and go down when it is cold.

When referring to temperatures, we usually speak about the day being hotter or the soup colder. This might lead to the erroneous notion that temperature "measures" heat. Instead, temperature indicates heat level and responds to heat increase or decrease, but it does not measure heat in the same way that a ruler measures length. Heat is a much more complex concept than one-dimensional length. Therefore, in conversations with students, say that we read the temperature from the thermometer (by measuring the length of the indicator fluid, for instance), we don't measure the amount of heat. This concept will be developed in science courses later in their schooling.

Some may think that students will be confused by the negative sign prevalent in weather forecasts during winter in Canada and the northern U.S. We believe that this exposure to the negative sign will not necessarily confuse them and provides a concrete reference when, in later years, they study and use negative numbers in dealing with money and other concepts. Describing the temperatures as above or below zero also makes the positive and negative signs more meaningful as mathematical ways of referring to numbers on either side of zero.

Realistic and relevant targets for temperature

Students will have a basic competence in using temperatures in practical situations if they are able:

See Activities 5.14 and 5.15.

1. To give the approximate temperature of certain situations, such as a warm summer day, an oven for baking pies, normal body temperature and what is considered to be a high fever, boiling water, an ice cube, and a winter day suitable for outdoor activity (or other common situations).
2. Given some common temperatures, to provide examples of situations that would match that information.
3. To read a common outdoor thermometer to the nearest five degrees (depending upon the thermometer scale).
4. To estimate the outdoor temperature to within five degrees.
5. To read, write, and speak the correct terminology of temperature (degrees).

Suggested activities

Activity 5.1 Class Estimation Challenge

This activity can always be included in the day's activities, whatever aspect of measurement is being considered. Focused on the measurement targets related to estimation, it aims to develop the student's sense of what it is that is being measured and the size of the units concerned. If structured carefully, it can also give low achievers some successful experience of collecting and organizing a set of data, displaying it in graphical form, and interpreting the results.

Materials
2-cm grid paper, glue, scissors, colored paper cut in 2-cm wide strips.

Estimating length (Length Targets 11 and 12)
For about eight days, begin each mathematics lesson by asking the class to make estimates for some length. For the first four days the lesson should begin with a quick review of the reference items for length, encouraging the children to memorize these and to use them for comparison. For the remaining four days, you may not need to remind them of the reference items.

Indicate or show to the children an item up to 200 cm long. Have each student write an estimate of its length on a slip of paper. Over eight days with one low-achieving class, Derek used the distance from his nose to his outstretched finger tip (101 cm), the length of his briefcase (43 cm), his height (183 cm), a student's height (142 cm), the width of a window-pane (50 cm), the height of the chalkboard (114 cm), the width of the door (84 cm) and the height of a desk (63 cm). The challenge to the class is to see if they can gradually make better and better estimates of length.

> The goal of this excellent cooperative activity is for everyone to improve at the task.

Handling the data

Collect the slips of paper with the estimates. Derek always makes a point of not disclosing the actual measurement at this stage, keeping the class in some suspense. A group of three students is given the responsibility of organizing and presenting the day's data in graphical form.

With low achievers, this process should be very carefully structured. First they put the slips of paper into piles, to determine how many estimates are in single figures, how many in the tens, how many in the twenties, the thirties, the forties and so on. We advise against attempting any more complicated groupings of the data than this.

The graphs drawn each day should follow a prescribed model: Derek provided the group on the first day with an example of what a finished graph should look like. The following is a suggestion to help low achievers quickly produce an effective and satisfying bar graph.

The horizontal axis is labelled "estimates" and the vertical axis "number of children." Label the vertical axis from 0 to 20 and the horizontal axis in tens, covering the range of estimates made by the class. To represent the number of students in each group, the graph-makers simply place a strip of colored paper along the vertical axis, mark carefully the length required, cut off this length, and glue it onto the chart. This technique produces a colorful bar graph in a way which is undoubtedly preferable to having the students draw the columns and color them with felt-tip pens.

How did we do?

When the group has finished drawing the data graph, they measure the actual length of the item. Show this by an arrow on the graph. At the end of the lesson, show the graph to the class and discuss with them how well they did in their estimating. Over the course of eight lessons we can expect to see the children gradually improving their estimating, demonstrated by a wall display of the graphs produced each day (see Figure 5.3). Challenge the class to give estimates within two groupings on either side of the actual length.

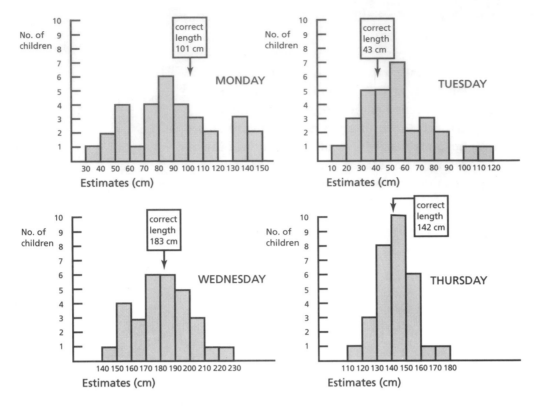

FIGURE 5.3 *Bar charts showing improvement in estimating lengths (for Activity 5.1)*

Estimating weight (Weight Targets 10 and 11)

You may repeat exactly the same estimation project for the topic of weight. This time, present an object each day which is passed around the class for the children to handle and to estimate the weight. If you have several identical objects, it will take less time for the children to make their estimates. The weights should be up to 1000 g. Examples might be: a text-book (240 g), a can of juice (360 g), a 500 mL carton of milk (450 g), and so on. Reviewing the reference items again, and having the students handle them, is important in the early stages of the project.

As with length, we propose that you tightly structure the handling of the data for low-achieving students. Group the estimates simply in hundreds: those up to a hundred, those in the one hundreds, the two hundreds, and so on. Once again, when the bar chart is completed, the children concerned can weigh the object to determine the actual weight and show this on their graph. The class challenge is to get all the estimates within two groups on either side of the actual weight.

Estimating capacity (Capacity Targets 9 and 10)

This follows exactly the same pattern as the weight project. Each day, show a container clearly to the class and ask them to estimate the capacity. Use a range of containers (bottles, cans, jars, vases, jugs). The reference items again play an important part in the process of estimating. As with weight, the estimates can be grouped in hundreds.

Estimating time (Time Target 5)

Since we do not have any reference items for time for direct comparison, as we do for length, weight, and capacity, start the first few lessons of the time topic by having the students count out loud, together with you, in seconds. Then each day, ask them to write down their estimates for a time interval in seconds, up to a minute. Do this by asking them to close their eyes and then, in silence, to estimate the number of seconds between clapping your hands once and clapping them a second time. Using the second-counter on a watch, give them a different time interval each day. For grouping the data, you may need to use a smaller interval size than 10 seconds in order to distribute the children's estimates across a number of groups. Five-second intervals (0-4, 5-9, 10-14, 15-19, ...) are usually appropriate.

You may want to give the students a practice item or two before estimating the item for which a bar graph will be constructed.

Some measurement games

All of the following games have been used successfully with low achievers for developing skills and concepts related to the targets for measurement. Use them to supplement the more conventional activities of measuring which are implied by and necessary for the targets.

Activity 5.2 Estimation Challenge

Materials

Two balance-type weighing devices; a supply of 100-g weights; a supply of plasticine, wood shavings, ball bearings, etc.; some light plastic jars.

Students practice measuring and estimating. Weight Targets 5 and 11, Length Targets 9 and 12.

Method

Two pairs of children play against each other. Behind screens, each pair measures out a quantity of the material available into a jar. The weight should be approximately a multiple of 100 grams. For example, one pair might choose to weigh 200 g of plasticine, while the other might weigh 800 g of ball bearings. Each team then estimates the weight of the contents of their opponent's jar. Award one point for estimating within 100 g, two points for getting it correct.

Variation

For length Targets 9 and 12, have the students use a meter ruler to draw lines of their chosen length. The opposing team has to estimate the length of each line to within 5 cm.

Activity 5.3 Kilogram Challenge

Materials

Various objects for weighing; a balance-type weighing device; a supply of 1-g, 10-g, and 100-g weights; and a calculator for each player.

Students practice estimation and multiplication in context. Weight Targets 5, 6 and 11. You may be surprised how quickly students develop the ability to make the estimates required for this game.

Method

Have one child act as umpire for this game. One player chooses an object. Each player then estimates how many of these objects are needed to weigh a kilogram or more. The estimates are written down by the umpire, who then weighs the object. If it is less than 50 g, all the players except the chooser win a point: this rule is to discourage players from choosing very light objects. If it is more than 50 g, the players use their calculators to determine the minimum number of the object needed to weigh 1 kg or more. A point is awarded to any player who estimated correctly.

For example, a paperback book might be chosen which weighs about 225 g. One player might estimate that four books would be needed to weigh more than 1 kg. From the calculator, he or she finds that 225 x 4 = 900. The player then tries 225 x 5, and from the result (1125) decides that five of the books would be required.

Variation

A messier version of this game, addressing capacity and liquid volume, can be played with water, sand (found in many kindergarten classrooms), or rice, and a supply of containers. Players estimate how many of each container would be required to exceed 1 L.

Activity 5.4 Time Cards

Materials

Individually or as a group, the students should prepare cards that match daily events and the times they occur. Figure 5.4 shows an example of a set of cards, using the events, 12-hour digital times, and the corresponding colloquial versions. Some children may prefer to draw the events rather than write them. Cut apart the matching cards and use them in various activities for practicing the ordering of times of the day. The set shown in Figure 5.4 produces 24 cards in eight different groups. A stopwatch may also be required.

> This small-group activity addresses Time Targets 10, 11, 13, 24, and 25. The students can also practice timing an activity by using a watch (Time Target 3).

asleep in bed	arrive at school	assembly	play time	having lunch	end of school	watching TV	going to bed
5:00 am	8:30 am	9:15 am	10:30 am	12:30 pm	3:45 pm	6:30 pm	9:00 pm
5 o'clock in the morning	half past 8 in the morning	quarter past 9 in the morning	half past 10 in the morning	half past 12 in the afternoon	quarter to 4 in the afternoon	half past 6 in the evening	9 o'clock in the evening

FIGURE 5.4 *Example of matching set for Activity 5.4: Time cards*

Method

Mix up the cards and challenge the students to reassemble the pattern by matching events and times. This can be done in turn with students timing each other using a stopwatch. Encourage students to compete with their own times, to see if they can get faster, rather than competing with each other. You could give special recognition to the most improved to reinforce the emphasis on personal growth and development.

Variations

Give one student the cards for the events, another the digital times, and a third the colloquial equivalents. Each student orders the cards separately, then they check to see if the three lines correspond.

Remove two rows of cards from the matching set, turn them face down, and mix them up. Students take turns to turn over two cards. If these give the same time of day, the student wins a point, keeps the cards, and gets another turn. If they do not match, they are turned face down again. Students may recognize this as a variation of the popular game "Concentration."

Activity 5.5 Messages to Order

Materials

A set of cards with times of the day written on one side and letters, spelling out a message, written on the other. Figure 5.5 gives an example.

More practice of ordering times of day. Time Target 25.

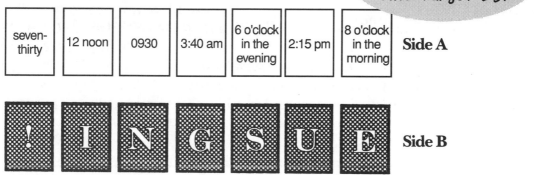

Figure 5.5 *Example of cards for Messages to Order (Activity 5.5)*

Method

Mix up the cards and give them to a student or a pair of students. They then arrange the cards to show the times in the correct order. When this is done, they turn them over to reveal a message. For example, the cards in Figure 5.5 give the message "GENIUS!"

Variations

Students enjoy making their own sets of these cards to give to other students to find the message. It is easier if the students compose the message first, then find times of day to use on the backs of the cards.

Activity 5.6 Timing Calculations

Materials

Two calculators, a stopwatch, and pencil and paper.

This activity gives practice in timing events using a stopwatch (Time Target 3) and in reading answers on a calculator.

Method

Students work in pairs. Using a calculator, each student prepares a two-option multiple choice test for the other. This is just a list of ten arithmetic operations, using two-digit numbers only, with a choice of a correct answer and an incorrect answer. The incorrect answer should always use the same digits but with the last two reversed. This forces the students to take great care when reading the digits on the calculator display. To get them started, give the students an example of the test. For instance, one player's test might begin with the following:

23 x 59	1375	1357
48 + 67	151	115
76 ÷ 43	1.7674418	1.7674481

The students then use the stopwatch, in turn, to time each other in answering the questions on their calculators, circling the correct option each time. A simple way of marking progress is to add an extra ten seconds for each incorrect answer and to check for the total score at the end. Other ways of judging growth can be devised by the teacher or the students themselves.

Activity 5.7 Calendar Puzzle

Materials

An old calendar with the months cut out separately and the names of the months removed.

Method

The problem is simply to reassemble the calendar: to decide which month is January, which is February, etc., and to arrange them in order. Students may need a hint that they should start by identifying February. Before they tackle this they should review the order of the months and the number of days in each month.

This puzzle is a good way to develop the students' grasp of the structure of a calendar (Time Targets 26 and 27).

Activity 5.8 Watch the Clock

Encourage students simply to keep their eye on the classroom clock and to become aware of the time of day.

Materials

The classroom clock (dial or digital, preferably both) and a set of cards with times of the day written on them. Some small rewards, such as candies.

This will improve students' ability to tell time (Time Targets 11, 12, 13, 15, 19, 20, 21, etc.).

Method

At the start of the school day (or a mathematics lesson), give each child a card with a time of day written on it. These could be at whatever level or in whatever form is appropriate to the individual child. For example, give some students something as simple as "10 o'clock," whereas others might get "2:15" or "ten past three." The normal lessons just continue for the day. However, the students are expected to keep an eye on the clock. When it gets to the time on their card, they hand the card to the teacher and collect their reward. If they miss their time, they miss the reward, but give them some appropriate explanation instead. It is amazing how quickly students pick up the skills of telling the time in this informal way, while we struggle to teach this through more formal exercises. Try this for a week and see the improvement! Use it periodically throughout the year for long-term retention and make the times progressively more difficult.

Variations

This activity might prove distracting and students could end up doing nothing but watching the clock so they don't miss their time. If this happens in your classroom, make some quick modifications so they can still collect their reward and receive recognition for reading the time correctly even if they become so enthralled with your lesson that they miss their time! Perhaps they could say something like, "It is ten minutes past my time."

Activity 5.9 Reading a Scale

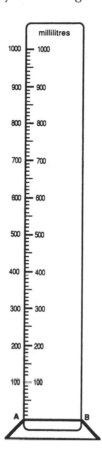

This simple yet effective activity helps students practice reading a scale for liquid volume (Capacity Target 5).

FIGURE 5.6 *Model for practice in reading a scale*

Materials

Various graduated measuring containers; two packs of cards: one pack with a different volume written on each card (e.g. 450 mL) and the other with cards that read either "more than" or "less than"; and rice, sand, or other material that pours. Brave teachers may want to use liquids!

Method

Each group of students fills its container to whatever point on the scale they wish and writes down the volume. One student, acting as umpire, checks these. The umpire then turns over a card from each pack, to reveal, for example, "less than 450 mL." Each group that has set their volume to less than 450 mL wins a point. The groups then dump and refill their containers. The umpire continues the game for an agreed-upon time, after which the scores are tallied.

Some purposeful activities in measurement contexts

Some low achievers find the exercises in the school mathematics program to be confusing and purposeless. These students stand their best chance of developing the knowledge, skills, and concepts of measurement by applying them in purposeful activities. Following the instructions for measuring ingredients in a recipe is the best example of a purposeful activity for achieving many of the weight and capacity targets. Our view is that practical cooking should be regarded as part of the mathematics curriculum, especially for low-achieving students. (See Chapter 6 for how to handle the concept of fractions often found in recipes.) The following are activities with some genuine purpose, involving length, time, or temperature.

Activity 5.10 Make a Box

Method

Identify some classroom items for which a storage box is required,
such as a set of calculators or a set of textbooks. A box to hold play
money, with separate compartments for 1¢, 10¢, and $1 coins or the various sizes of bills, would also be very useful. Students, working in pairs, undertake to make the various boxes. When completed, use the boxes (even if some require reinforcement), so that the activity is genuinely purposeful.

Length Targets 7, 9, and 16

To build a box, students have to make a number of mathematical decisions, both spatial and numerical. For example, they must decide on the layout of the materials in the box (are the 24 calculators stacked in 4 rows of 6, or 3 rows of 8, or how?) and the positioning of flaps. To get some ideas about how boxes are made, the students could take a few boxes apart and examine them.

The students should start by making a prototype from paper and tape. This will involve measuring the dimensions of the materials, drawing lines and right angles accurately, deciding on flaps, and possibly doing some calculations. One group of low achievers, making a box for 24 calculators, measured the width of one calculator to be 7 cm, used the calculator to multiply 7 by 24, and decided that the box had to be 168 cm long. They did not get far with their prototype before deciding that this was not the best solution. Once students build a successful prototype (after, perhaps, modifying it appropriately), they can construct the box with cardboard and glue.

Activity 5.11 Arranging the Classroom

Method

What is the best way of arranging the furniture in the classroom?
Ask groups of students to solve this problem. Accept the best
arrangements and try them out for a day or two, so that the activity is
genuinely purposeful. The students could produce a scale drawing of the classroom showing the fixed positions of doors and windows and their proposals for the arrangement of the furniture.

Length Targets 6, 9, and 15

To be suitable for low achievers, structure this activity carefully. If a scale of 1:10 is used (where 10 cm on the paper represents 1 m in the room), students will require a piece of paper 60 cm by 80 cm for a classroom 6 m by 8 m. This is larger than the normal large-size squared paper, so the children will need to stick two pieces together. (A scale of 1:100 would be too small.) Note that Length Target 15 treats simple one-to-one scales. However if you use squared paper marked in centimeters, with larger 10-cm squares highlighted, the students can use the length of one of these larger squares to represent one meter in the room. If they use 30-meter tape-measures marked in meters and tenths of a meter, they might also be able to cope with the idea that each extra little bit of a meter is represented by the length of one of the smaller squares on the squared paper.

Suggest that they make scale drawings to represent tables and other furniture, also using the 1:10 scale. They measure the tables in centimeters (e.g., 60 cm by 80 cm) and then draw these on millimeter-squared paper. They do not have to know how to handle millimeters, just to use the idea that one centimeter of table length is represented by the length of one of the little squares on the paper. Each piece of scale furniture should be cut out and labeled.

Clearly, other important spatial concepts are involved in the final process of deciding how to fit the scale drawings of the furniture into the plan of the room.

Activity 5.12 Timetables

Several Time Targets.

	Monday	Tuesday	Wednesday	Thursday	Friday
9:15 am					
9:45 am					
10:00 am					
10:15 am					
10:30 am					
10:45 am					
11.00 am					
11:15 am					
11:30 am					
11:45 am					
12 noon					

FIGURE **5.7** *Chart for personal timetable (Activity 5.12)*

Method
When you find you need a timetable for your students, you could ask them to devise one. With low achievers, you will need to prepare for and structure this task carefully to allow for their limitations.

A useful preparatory activity is to have each student keep a personal record of how they spend their time at school for a week, using a chart like the one shown in Figure 5.7. Every fifteen minutes you could stop the class and ask them to fill in an entry on the chart. This may sound tedious, but by the end of a week the children will have developed a surprising confidence in handling time concepts. They will also have become clock-watchers, which, as far as achieving the time targets is concerned, is not a bad thing. Some students may then be able to extend the activity and keep a record of how they spend their time out of school as well. You could encourage this as a homework project in coop-eration with parents and caregivers.

After a week of time-recording, they can tackle problems of timetabling. For example, working in pairs, using the same kind of structured grid shown in Figure 5.4, they could devise the timetable for a day (or several days) at school. You might want to impose certain constraints on the timetables. The finished timetables could be put on display and the whole class could gently critique each one and try to decide which one to adopt. Different groups could devise the timetable for a sports or entertainment event, or a class trip. Each of these assignments could be peer-critiqued and chosen as a class decision. Some interesting hybrids may also emerge.

Activity 5.13 Programming a VCR

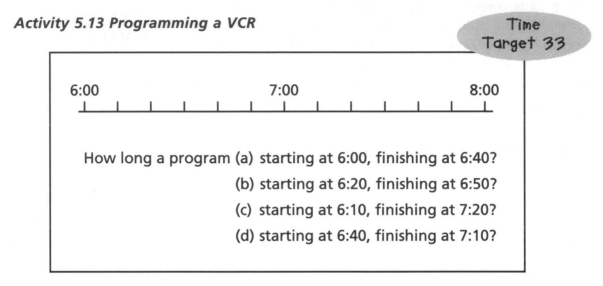

FIGURE 5.8 *Preparation for programming a VCR (Activity 5.13)*

Method

One group of teachers who worked with Derek on the problems facing low achievers in mathematics decided that this is the ultimate target for teaching time. If the student can successfully program a VCR to record several shows transmitted over several days, then many of the time targets will have been achieved. If we want certain programs recorded in a particular week (say, for use in school), then setting the VCR is a job for our low-achieving students, not one for the school secretary.

To lead up to this skill, one teacher found it helpful to give a group of students a worksheet like the one shown in Figure 5.8. Before setting the VCR, the students read the information in published TV guides and recorded their plans in a table with these headings:

Program Title
Channel
Day
Start time
Finish time
Length in minutes

Variations

Students may find that setting an alarm clock (either digital or analog) is a good intermediate step to programming a VCR.

Activity 5.14 Common Reference Points

Create a large class-size thermometer with a scale marked every five degrees from -40 to +120. With the students, label some of the temperatures with corresponding events such as boiling water, a very cold winter day, normal body temperature etc. Then, ask each student to commit these to memory. Without looking at the class thermometer, students should be able to remember the temperature of the events and vice versa.

> Temperature Targets 1, 2, and 5.

Activity 5.15 Drawing a Temperature Graph

This excellent, long-term project has connections with science, social studies, and data management in the mathematics curriculum. In the context of the changing seasons, the notation and language for negative temperatures may be introduced and reinforced.

> Temperature Targets 3–5.

Materials

Outdoor thermometer mounted in the shade by the classroom window (or other student-accessible location), large graph paper.

Method

Each day at a specific time, a pair of students reads the outdoor thermometer and reports to the class. They, or other students, then mark the graph appropriately. Note that students are instructed to "read" the thermometer. Do not ask them to see how hot or how cold it is outside. This will help avoid the confusion of thinking that they are measuring heat!

Key teaching points

- Work with real items to perform actual measurement.
- Establish reference items: familiar objects with easily memorized measurements which become references for other items.
- Use estimation to develop common sense understandings of measures.

QUESTIONS FOR DISCUSSION WITH COLLEAGUES

1. Can you improve on our suggestions for reference items for length, weight, and capacity? Might others be more relevant to your students?
2. Give other explanations of the students' incorrect response to the conservation of volume task shown in Figure 5.1. How might a student's grasp of the principles of conservation of length, weight, and liquid volume be recognized through activities embedded in more meaningful contexts?
3. How could Activity 5.2 be adapted for capacity and liquid volume and Activity 5.3 for length?
4. Devise some other games using calendars (see Activity 5.7) which could be used to help students achieve Time Targets 26-29.
5. How might the games and activities we have presented be altered to take on a more cooperative nature?

6 Confidence with Numbers and Operations: A Vital Goal in Numeracy

A vital goal in numeracy for students is need to develop a network of understanding of number operations — to make connections between the manipulation of the symbols and the corresponding pictures, language, and concrete situations (refer to Figure 2.1). Only this basis of understanding of number operations gives any meaning to the knowledge and skills of arithmetic.

FEATURES OF THIS CHAPTER

- fuzzy regions of understanding and numeracy
- an analysis of operations
- addition and subtraction relationships
- multiplication and division relationships
- suggested learning targets (cross-referenced to activities)
  - understanding number operations
  - number knowledge and mental arithmetic
  - calculation skills
  - handling big numbers
- suggested activities (cross-referenced to targets)
- estimation activities
- key teaching points

Fuzzy regions

David, aged 10, a low achiever in mathematics, was able to write the correct answer in the first of the following two questions but he was stumped by the second, even with a calculator available:

- Jim has 3¢. The book costs 5¢. Jim needs _ ¢ more
- Jim has 59¢. The book costs 147¢. Jim needs _ ¢ more

Although he can use the relationship between 3 and 5 and his understanding of the structure of the problem to answer the first question, he does not recognize what he is doing as subtraction. Indeed, since David answers the question by counting from 3 to 5 on his fingers, he appears to be doing an addition. But the structure of the problem is, nevertheless, the relationship of subtraction as reversing addition in the context of money. Given the larger numbers of the second problem, he is unable to recognize that a subtraction is required. He actually presses the addition key on his calculator and looks puzzled by the result.

This is a familiar scenario. Children can often solve small number problems with structures from any of the different operations delineated in this chapter without explicitly being aware of the operation concerned. Somewhere between the small number problem they can solve and the large number problem which they cannot solve, even with a calculator available, lies what we call the "fuzzy region."

David was given a worksheet with the following series of graded problems, all with the same reversing addition structure. He had a calculator and knew that he could use it whenever he wanted to.

1. Jim has 3¢. The book costs 5¢. Jim needs _ ¢ more
2. Jim has 3¢. The book costs 7¢. Jim needs _ ¢ more
3. Jim has 5¢. The book costs 8¢. Jim needs _ ¢ more
4. Jim has 13¢. The book costs 17¢. Jim needs _ ¢ more
5. Jim has 13¢. The book costs 27¢. Jim needs _ ¢ more
6. Jim has 32¢. The book costs 47¢. Jim needs _ ¢ more
7. Jim has 38¢. The book costs 71¢. Jim needs _ ¢ more
8. Jim has 23¢. The book costs 61¢. Jim needs _ ¢ more
9. Jim has 53¢. The book costs 92¢. Jim needs _ ¢ more
10. Jim has 59¢. The book costs 147¢. Jim needs _ ¢ more

David's fuzzy region was around Questions 4 and 5. Questions 1, 2 and 3 he could answer from his knowledge of the number relationships or just by counting on his fingers. Clearly, he understood the logic of the questions, but did not associate their structure with subtraction. As he got into the fuzzy region, where he could not quite cope with the numbers involved, he took the calculator and started exploring various possibilities. Because the numbers were almost within his grasp he soon recognized which sequence of keys gave the right answer. So he actually discovered for himself that the operation of subtraction was appropriate to this structure, and he quickly applied this to the remaining questions. It is, of course, important that he reinforce this learning by articulating what he discovered in conversation with his teacher or other students, otherwise the experience is unlikely to be connected to any coherent network of understanding.

Helen, age 11, was working on the relationship of division as reversing multiplication in the context of money. She had a calculator available to help answer the following series of questions:

1. How many pieces of candy costing 2¢ can I buy with 8¢?
2. How many pieces of candy costing 3¢ can I buy with 9¢?
3. How many pieces of candy costing 5¢ can I buy with 10¢?
4. How many pieces of candy costing 10¢ can I buy with 40¢?
5. How many pieces of candy costing 5¢ can I buy with 20¢?
6. How many pieces of candy costing 4¢ can I buy with 12¢?
7. How many pieces of candy costing 6¢ can I buy with 24¢?
8. How many pieces of candy costing 8¢ can I buy with 40¢?
9. How many pieces of candy costing 8¢ can I buy with 64¢?
10. How many pieces of candy costing 12¢ can I buy with 96¢?

Likewise, Helen could answer the earlier questions, but did not associate them with division. So she did not know what calculation to enter for Question 10. Her fuzzy region was around Questions 5 and 6. At this stage, she turned to the calculator and discovered for herself that "20 ÷ 5" and "12 ÷ 4" gave what she could recognize as correct answers, and then went on to apply division to the remaining questions correctly.

Teachers, teacher associates, and parents can use series of examples like these for any of the classes of problems outlined in this chapter, with calculators available when the numbers get too big to handle easily. Often these examples will assist students to move from their confidence with small numbers, through the fuzzy region, and into the realms of uncertainty. In this way they can discover the mathematical structure involved for themselves, then articulate it and make it explicit.

These targets address the general ability to find the correct answer using a calculator.

Because of these fuzzy regions, it helps students if they actually manipulate concrete materials and learn to identify when a problem is addition, subtraction, multiplication, or division. The above examples of fuzzy regions also illustrate the power of the calculator in allowing students to focus on the elements of the problem rather than on the complexity of the paper and pencil algorithms. We believe that the two central goals for our students are learning the fundamental structures of questions involving the four operations and learning to use the calculator effectively.

In this technological (calculator) age, it is no longer important that a student be able to do the actual calculations. Instead, our first three specific targets state that students should be able:

1. To state what keys should be entered on a calculator in order to solve a practical problem for each operation — addition, subtraction, multiplication, and division — in any appropriate context.

A key skill for all aspects of numeracy is judging how reasonable an answer is. See Activities 6.20, 6.21, 6.22, 6.23.

2. To enter the numbers correctly.
3. To judge the reasonableness of the answer by estimating and interpreting the answer relative to the problem and calculator display.

These three targets are crucial for two reasons: (1) they are useful and (2) they form an important component in the development of the student's understanding of number operations. Knowing what calculation to do and which keys to enter on the calculator in all possible practical situations is surely a fundamental component of numeracy for it enables students to cope confidently with the numerical demands of everyday life. It is also an indication of real understanding, since choosing the operation involves a direct connection between the symbols of arithmetic and the corresponding concrete situations. In our work with low achievers we have made these our primary targets. Far from being a trivial exercise, this has always proved to be a major undertaking. It is so important that we devote as much time to it as necessary.

Some may prefer that students work out the answer using paper and pencil methods rather than relying on the calculator, claiming that it is better exercise to do the arithmetic by hand. While it is true that the algorithms give practice in basic facts, the algorithms seldom enhance understanding. In fact, the long process of trying to do the calculations may actually detract from the problem-solving process by directing inappropriate time and energy to the computational aspects of the situation. When students use the calculator judiciously and in context, they are able to concentrate on the reasoning aspects of the problem — the parts a machine can't handle.

We prefer that teachers find more interesting and rewarding ways of practicing the basic facts than by making students work through pages of questions that demand the application of algorithms. Furthermore, when students use estimation skills to determine the reasonableness of the answer, they are employing many basic facts, often in their heads. We know that students become more competent with their basic facts because of the meaningfulness of the practice embedded in the estimation and reasoning processes.

> Estimating to judge how reasonable the answer is provides excellent practice of basic number facts.

Although many teachers accept that "knowing what operation to do" is an important target, particularly for low achievers, it is very rare for a teacher (or a school or school board) to tackle this in a systematic way. So, our targets and activities in this chapter try to cover precisely those situations in which students have to choose the operation.

An analysis of operations

To help analyze the task which faces us, we have outlined below what we mean by contexts and relationships. We provide examples of the practical problems in each of these relationships where the student must decide what keys should be entered on the calculator to solve the problem (see Figures 6.1 and 6.5). Students should be exposed to different types of problems in a systematic way and be able to choose the correct operation when confronted with any number of addition, subtraction, multiplication, and division questions or problems. (Interested readers are directed to literature on learning concepts such as Merrill et al., 1992.)

Contexts

First, notice that the learning targets refer to "any appropriate context." Calculations may need to be done in many different contexts, such as those aspects of students' lives identified in Figure 2.2 as "meaningful contexts." The numbers which turn up in these situations are usually attached to a set of things (most frequently to money) or sometimes to

a measurement of some kind. Therefore, we analyze this problem of choosing the operation in terms of the following categories of contexts:
- sets of things
- money
- measurement: length and distance, weight, capacity and liquid volume
- time

In this analysis, we are concerned only with developing the student's ability to choose the appropriate operation for a calculation which might arise in these contexts. This assumes the relevant knowledge, skills, and concepts associated with measurement which were considered in Chapter 5.

Relationships

Part of the difficulty here (see also Chapter 3) is that the student has to learn to connect the correct mathematical symbol (+, −, ÷ or ×) to a great variety of different situations. These situations vary not just in their contexts, but also in the actual mathematical structure of the problem and the logical relationships between its numerical components. Each operation has several different relationships, of which the following are considered in our analysis:

- addition as collecting
- addition as adding on
- subtraction as partitioning
- subtraction as taking away
- subtraction as comparing
- subtraction as reversing addition
- multiplication as repeated collecting
- division as equal sharing
- division as repeated subtraction
- division as reversing multiplication

Classes of problems: addition and subtraction

The classes of problems shown in Figure 6.1 vary greatly in the extent to which they are realistic and purposeful. Some classes contain problems which are genuine, can be presented in a practical mode, and are likely to be meaningful to students. But for other classes the kinds of problems are rather artificial, can only be presented in story mode, or are likely less purposeful for the students than one might hope. However, even these less purposeful or artificial problems contribute to the building up of connections between the symbols, the associated language, and the classes of problems. These connections are very important in the development of the student's understanding of the operations. Emphasize the more meaningful situations first and then students can move more confidently into unfamiliar or more abstract situations.

For each example, ask the students, "What do you enter on your calculator to solve this problem? Why? How do you decide if your answer is close (estimation)?" If they can answer these questions, you have sufficient evidence that they have attained the two central goals for their work in operations.

FIGURE 6.1 *Classes of Addition and Subtraction Problems*

CONTEXTS AND RELATIONSHIPS	SETS	MONEY	MEASUREMENT	TIME
Addition as Collecting	"Given the number of students in each of these two classes, how many students altogether?"	"How much money was raised by two classes in a fund-raising event if one raised $25.95 and the other raised $33.22?"	"By road, Edmonton to Saskatoon is 546 km, and Saskatoon to Winnipeg is 793 km. How far is Edmonton to Winnipeg, via Saskatoon?"	"It usually takes 95 minutes by car travelling at the speed limit to go from Grand Forks, North Dakota to Emerson, Manitoba, and then a further 75 minutes to get to Winnipeg. How long is the whole trip?"
Addition as Adding On		"A meal at the restaurant is listed as $6.95. If the tax is $0.70, what is the total price?"	"A student stands on a bathroom scale and records her weight; if she then picks up a back-pack weighing 12 kg, what would she weigh then?"	"A student indicates how old her father is. How old will he be in 38 years?"
Subtraction as Partitioning	"There are 218 children in the school. If 126 bring their lunches to school, how many do not?"	"If I give a ten-dollar bill for something that costs $7.85, how much change should I get?"	"If I pour 150 mL from a 500-mL carton of milk, how much is left?"	"Grandma is 82 years old; she has been married for 57 years. How long was she single?"
Subtraction as Taking Away		"The price of an item costing $7.25 is reduced by $1.85; what is the new price?"	"A student stands on a bathroom scale and records his weight; if he lost 10 kg, what would he weigh then?"	"It is now my birthday in 1999 and I was born 11 years ago; in what year was I born?"
Subtraction as Comparing	"Two students compare their collections of marbles. Jo has 29 and Pat has 54. How many more does Pat have than Jo? How many fewer does Jo have than Pat?"	"One brand of running shoe is priced at $75.99 a pair, another at $47.25 a pair. How much more expensive is the first brand? How much less expensive is the second brand?"	"The distance between Vancouver (British Columbia) and Tacoma (Washington) is 173 miles and between Vancouver and Everett is 118 miles. How much farther is Tacoma than Everett? How much nearer is Everett than Tacoma?"	"A trip takes 48 minutes by subway train and 65 minutes by bus. How much longer is the journey by bus? How much quicker is it by subway?"
Subtraction as Reversing Addition	"A student counts 87 pencils in a pot. If we need 140 pencils for the whole school, how many more must we buy?"	"Cathy has $57 in savings but a bike costs $95. How much must she earn so that she can buy the bike?"	"A linebacker on the local football team wants to reach his target weight of 102 kg. If he now weighs 99 kg, how much weight must he put on?"	"I was told that the books would arrive in 28 days and so far I've waited for 15 days. How much longer must I wait?"

The structure of the problem is not affected by the actual numbers used or whether measurements are given in metric or imperial units.

Teaching addition and subtraction relationships

Students need to be exposed to the various kinds of addition and subtraction questions but need not remember the name of the question types. These names are for your benefit only. Subtraction is actually a far more complex operation for students to understand than addition. It involves learning to connect the symbol with a wide range of classes of problems. This is where a calculator is a real aid to the development of understanding, because it enables the student to focus on the structure of the problems rather than the mechanics of the arithmetic. We should note also that, since subtraction is a non-commutative operation ("a – b" is not the same thing as "b – a"), students must learn to enter the numbers in the correct key sequence. In most practical problems this means entering the larger number first.

"Take away" often means subtraction; but subtraction is much more besides.

Priorities in Teaching Addition and Subtraction

Begin teaching addition and subtraction relationships using situations that are familiar or can be made concrete with materials or manipulatives. For example, subtraction as partitioning is a very significant component of the student's understanding of operations and one that merits high priority. Comparing things is a fundamental process by which we make sense of our experiences, so all four contexts generate interesting problems. A wide range of important language is used in this relationship, such as shorter, longer, taller, nearer, farther, higher, lower, wider, and narrower. It could be argued, therefore, that subtraction as partitioning is the most significant subtraction relationship and should be given greater emphasis than the others.

Children tend to respond in a stimulus-response fashion to key words rather than to the logical structure in questions (see Nesher & Teubal, 1975; Hope, 1990). Therefore concrete materials should be used to develop understanding. By manipulating small sets of materials, students notice the relationship between what needs to be added and the operation of subtraction. The concrete materials give them a visual and tactile representation of the operation which they can then verbalize and compare to the calculator operation. Also, with calculators available, students can focus on the logical structure of the problem and not be distracted by the complexity of the arithmetic involved when using larger numbers.

Subtraction as partitioning is so similar to addition as adding on that it poses great difficulties for some students. To find what must be added, it seems odd that we have to press the subtraction key on the calculator.

We should not try to establish a particular mathematical structure in the student's understanding by using unfamiliar contexts about which they may be hesitant. First, establish the relationships of addition and subtraction in the contexts of money and sets. Using these two contexts side by side ensures that the multi-embodiment principle (see

Chapter 2) is at work. Once the students are confidently choosing the operation for each relationship of addition and subtraction in these two contexts, we could move these operations into the less familiar measuring contexts in order to deepen or extend their understanding.

Estimation strategies for addition and subtraction

NCTM (1989) stresses the importance of estimation for determining the reasonableness of results.

Estimates are quick and simple, and give people an approximate or basic solution in a situation. To increase speed, accuracy is deliberately sacrificed. This is done by eliminating unnecessary details (complex numbers) and working with simplified numbers. But estimates also need a certain degree of accuracy in order to help us make sense of our world. Students need to understand the principle that estimating involves a balance between speed, accuracy, and understanding. It may take many experiences with estimates and working with realistic problems in meaningful settings before students find the balance suitable for most situations.

Some students may not be comfortable with estimating answers, especially when doing math! If that is the case, take some time to explore the role of estimation in daily life. Have students interview parents, neighbors, and other adults to find out when and where they use estimation at home, at work, and when relaxing. Give students a set of situations involving numbers and ask which need an exact answer and which need only an estimate.

Estimation activities in a variety of situations and contexts should take place in class every day. When children are asked to give an estimation as well as calculate the exact answer for worksheet questions, they learn that estimating is extra work with no real purpose. Instead, point out the usefulness of the skill and organize activities that make valid use of estimates. A good reason for estimation is to determine the reasonableness of the result as a check on the calculator display when the students are using calculators.

We present several specific methods for estimating. They can be taught and reinforced alongside the activities presented in this and other chapters. However, we urge you to accept a range of answers and methods from students. Some students may develop very informal yet elegant ways of estimating. Encourage students to discuss the reasons for their choices of methods. Use the language of estimation, such as close, about, just about, nearly, a little more or a little less, and between. If an estimate is a long way from the exact answer, you may want to ask which estimation method is more appropriate (or which gives us the most useful information).

This example comes from the class of addition as adding on: "Find the total amount of money raised by two classes in a fund-raising event if one raised $25.95 and the other raised $33.27." Round to $25.00 and $35.00 and add. Check the estimate against the exact addition on the calculator. Have students predict whether the calculator display will be a little less or a little more than the estimate.

Front-End Methods of Estimation

This simple estimation method for addition or subtraction can be used when most of the numbers have the same number of digits. First, the front-end digits are added or subtracted and then an adjustment is made for the remaining digits (see Figure 6.2). Note that many adjustments could be made, especially for large numbers. Each adjustment increases accuracy but decreases speed. Reinforce the notion that estimating involves a trade-off between speed and accuracy and accept a range of responses from students. The crucial question for students is, "Did my estimation help me to understand the problem and give me some confidence that my calculator-assisted answer was correct?"

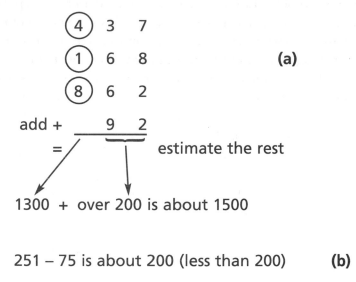

(a)

251 − 75 is about 200 (less than 200) **(b)**

FIGURE 6.2 *Front-end estimating for addition and subtraction*

Rounding Methods of Estimation

Rounding is a common method of estimation and actually compensates for some of the inaccuracy. The skill of rounding must be well understood and mastered. We suggest that practice in rounding be embedded in estimation, the meaningful and purposeful context for it, rather than taught as an isolated skill. If adding only a few numbers, they could be rounded and added mentally. For a longer list, low achievers may want to round and rewrite each number on paper as they go (see Figure 6.3). We recommend that all the numbers be rounded to the same place value, where possible. This means that some small numbers may be completely left out (i.e., rounded to zero). Rounding to zero may be a difficult concept for some students and reinforcing experiences will be needed.

(a) 136 + 81 + 205 is about
    100 + 100 + 200 = 400

(b) 212   200
      367   400
       27   000
      109   100
    is about 700

FIGURE 6.3 *Rounding to the nearest 100*

Using Compatible Numbers for Estimation

When adding a long list of numbers it may be useful to look for those that are compatible — that make a multiple of 10 or 100. These can be grouped to produce an easy and accurate estimate (see Figure 6.4 (a)).

For subtraction (and for additions with only two numbers), the students may be able to achieve speed and accuracy by changing, not rounding one of the numbers. These compatible numbers are then easier to subtract. In subtraction, it is better to change the number being subtracted (since making adjustments to the estimated answer is easier if this number has been changed). As in Figure 6.4(b), subtract and adjust. Adjusting is not always necessary. For many questions, an estimate without adjusting will give the students confidence that they are in the right range with their calculator-assisted computation, and this was our original goal. To adjust, determine if too much was subtracted, then put some back (increase the size of the estimate); if too little was subtracted, take some more away (decrease the size of the estimate).

(a)

(b)

$$677 - 253 \longrightarrow 677 - 277 = 400$$
$$\text{(or 420 adjusted)}$$

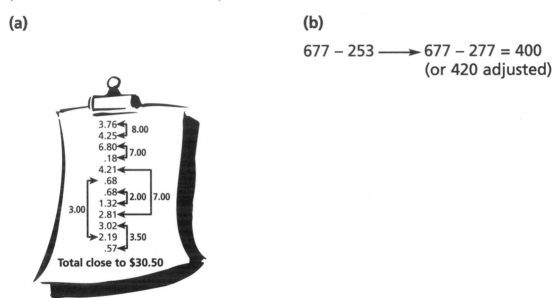

FIGURE **6.4** *Using compatible numbers to estimate*

Teaching multiplication and division relationships

Multiplication relationships

The relationship of multiplication as repeated collecting refers to those situations where multiplication is used to calculate "so many groups of so many." This is an extension of the relationship of addition as collecting, and an example is the total cost of a number of articles at a given price.

The relationship of multiplication as scaling is not used in this book. In this relationship, a given quantity is increased by a scale factor. For example, to increase the price of an article by 20%, multiplication by the scale factor 1.20 is required. Although this relationship is important for numeracy, its practical problems are usually too difficult for low-achieving students in this age range, so we omitted it from our analysis.

Note that the two numbers in a multiplication statement cannot refer to the same kind of thing, in contrast to addition and subtraction where they must. For example, you can only add a weight to a weight. It is meaningless to add the weight of an article to its price! But it is equally meaningless to multiply a weight by a weight, or the number in one set of counters by the number in another set.

Consider a multiplication statement, such as "3 x 4." If the "3" refers to the number of apples in a bag, the "4" cannot also refer to a number of apples. It must refer to something else, such as the number of bags, the price of a single apple, or the weight of a single apple. Thus, to classify multiplication problems we need to consider pairs of contexts. Those pairs which could be used to generate appropriate multiplication problems are as follows:

- sets x sets
- sets x money
- sets x length or distance, weight, volume or capacity, or time
- money x length or distance, weight, volume or capacity, or time
- average speed x time
- length x length

Figure 6.5 gives examples illustrating the classes of multiplication problems used in this book. Once again, the question to be asked for each problem is: what keys should be entered on the calculator and why? The student must learn to recognize that the logical structure of the problem requires the selection of the multiplication key. Since multiplication, like addition, is a commutative operation ("a x b" gives the same result as "b x a"), the key sequence in which the two numbers are entered in the calculator does not matter.

As with addition and subtraction, multiplication classes vary in their ability to generate purposeful, relevant, genuine, and practical problems. We take this into account when we determine the priorities for each class.

Division relationships

Most problems of division as equal sharing, as shown in Figure 6.5, have an answer that represents a set or portion. One of the two numbers in the problem is often attached to the word "per" (or some equivalent phrase).

The division as repeated subtraction relationship refers to situations where "12 ÷ 4" is interpreted as "find how many times 4 can be taken away from 12 until there's nothing left." Since this has a very similar logical structure to the reverse-of-multiplication relationship, with just a slightly different question being asked, we have not included it in our analysis.

In the division as ratio relationship, division is used to compare two quantities, not to find the difference between them (as in the comparison relationship of subtraction). It involves finding the ratio between them, e.g., comparing the salaries of two people earning \$45 000 and \$54 000 by dividing one by the other (54 000 ÷ 45 000) to determine the ratio of their salaries. We then say that one person earns 1.2 times as much as the other. This is a difficult relationship of division, which uses a rather abstract notion, and causes considerable problems for many adults. Even though it is essentially just an extension of the relationship of division as reversing multiplication, we think that it is too complex to be tackled systematically with low achievers in the 8–12 age range. We have already identified many types of problems in which the student has to learn to recognize the operation required, so they already have quite a challenge before them.

Division as reversing multiplication includes many common classes of problems. These are outlined in Figure 6.5.

Multiplication, division, and relationships between units

When faced with problems involving relationships between units in a given context, particularly those of time, we must help students recognize when multiplication or division are required. For example, consider the following problems:

"How many days are there in 12 weeks?"
"How many hours are there in 3 days?"

Here, multiplication is required because each problem can be interpreted as a kind of repeated collecting. For example, "12 weeks" is considered as "12 sets of 7 days." Conversely, using the reverse-of-multiplication relationship, the student should recognize the following as requiring a division:

"How many weeks is 350 days?"
"How many hours is 240 minutes?"
"How many minutes is 3000 seconds?"

Another difficult relationship involves converting units between the imperial and metric systems, such as converting a weight from pounds to kilograms, or a volume of gasoline from liters to gallons. Similar too are the problems of currency exchange, such as converting a sum of money from US dollars to yen or euros. We do not normally expect to include problems of these kinds with low achievers in the 8–12 age range, although they should be able to use conversion charts in practical situations that require conversions.

Teaching multiplication and division

Clearly, helping our students to learn to choose the operations of multiplication and division in all the types of problems outlined in Figure 6.5 is a big task. As well, because some types are more significant than others, we must determine priorities for these as was done for addition and subtraction. We should establish the structures of the various relationships first in the more familiar contexts of sets and money, before moving students into the less familiar measuring contexts. Furthermore, since children appear to find the relationship of division as equal sharing more meaningful and accessible than multiplication (Brown, 1981), we suggest that you teach multiplication and division as reversing multiplication at the same time in the various contexts.

When the calculator display has digits after the decimal point, these must be interpreted as items left over which can usually be ignored. Some calculators which show a remainder when giving the result of a division operation would be especially helpful for our students. For example: "100 marbles to be shared among 7 children; how many marbles do they each get?" (Calculator result: $100 \div 7 = 14.285714$; the answer is 14 marbles each with some left over. A calculator that gives a remainder would show that the answer is 14 marbles each with 2 left over.) The context is important. In many sharing problems such as this one, the objects cannot be divided and shared out. In others problems such as dividing a number of cookies, the remaining objects can be partitioned.

Estimation strategies for multiplication and division

When using the front-end method for multiplication or division, use just the first digit of both numbers, placing zeros in the other positions of the number (see Figure 6.6(a)). For

FIGURE 6.5 *Classes of Multiplication and Division Problems*

MULTIPLICATION AS REPEATED COLLECTING

Sets x sets: "There are 12 sets of reading books in the classroom, with 24 books in each set. How many books altogether?"	**Sets x money:** "How much will it cost to take 25 children to the safari park if it costs $4.50 per child?"	**Sets x measurements:** "My trip to work and home again each day is 28 km. How many kilometers do I travel in 20 days?"	**Money x measurements:** "A person can earn about $12.00 an hour delivering newspapers. How much can one earn in 5 hours?"	**Average speed x time:** "I can drive about 80 kph in my car on the highway; about how far can I go in 6 hours?"	**Length x length:** "If there are 10 rows of 5 chairs each, how many chairs are there in all?"

DIVISION AS EQUAL SHARING

Sets ÷ sets: "If 60 children are divided into 5 teams; how many are there in each team?"	**Money ÷ sets:** "A pack of 6 batteries costs $5.10; how much is this per battery? Compare this price with a pack of 8 batteries costing $6.50."	**Sets ÷ money:** "You can buy 1000 cards for $20; how many cards is this per dollar?"	**Measurements ÷ sets:** "Share a 1500-mL jug of lemonade equally among 12 children."	**Money ÷ measurements:** "Find the cost per ounce for an 8-ounce box of cereal at $1.65. (Compare this with the cost per ounce for a 10-ounce box of cereal at $1.80.)" "If $480 is to be repaid in 12 monthly installments, how much per month?"	**Measurements ÷ money:** "Find how many grams of corn flakes you get per penny if a 250-g box costs 80¢; compare this with how many grams per penny you get in a 750-g box costing 180¢."

DIVISION AS REVERSING MULTIPLICATION

Sets ÷ sets: "If there are 200 children in the school to be put into classes of 25, how many classes are there?"	**Money ÷ money:** "How many contributions of $2.50 do we need to raise $100.00?"	**Measurements ÷ measurements:** "How many lengths of 2 ft. can be cut from an 8 ft. length of wood?"	**Per:** "Potatoes cost $0.18 per pound. How many pounds of potatoes can I buy if I spend $5.04?" (Money is divided by money per pound, and the result represents a weight.)	**Distance ÷ average speed:** "How long will it take me to travel 270 km if I drive about 75 kph?" (Distance is divided by average speed (distance per hour), and the answer represents a time.)	**Distance ÷ time:** "Including rest stops, it takes me five hours to travel 446 km. About how many kph do I travel on average?"

some division questions, it may be easier to use a cumulative multiplication method for estimating the answer. For example, in the question 4693 ÷ 6, the students might begin with 100 sixes (600) and keep adding them until they get close to 4000. In this case, it would take six 600s to make 3600, seven 600s to make 4200, and eight 600s to make 4800. Eight 600s gives us a more reasonable answer and is equivalent to 8 x 100 sixes or 800 sixes. If it takes 800 sixes to make 4800, then the estimate for the division problem is 800. However, this reasoning may be difficult for low achievers and should be approached cautiously. Begin with smaller numbers and ensure understanding before moving on. Many activities in this chapter will help to develop the number sense needed to estimate answers for division questions.

When estimating for multiplication, accuracy can be greatly compromised by rounding. Rounding one number up and the other down may compensate (see Figure 6.6). Students would definitely benefit from experimenting with various approaches to see which gives a more accurate estimate without sacrificing simplicity and speed.

(a) 578 x 76 is about 600 x 80 = 48 000 **(reasonable estimate)**
   (or) is about 600 x 70 = 42 000 **(more accurate estimate)**

(b) $6.42 x 33 is about $6.00 x 30 = $180.00 **(reasonable estimate)**
   (or) is about $7.00 x 30 = $210.00 **(more accurate estimate)**

FIGURE 6.6 *Estimation examples for multiplication*

Specific targets for low achievers

(See Targets 1 to 3 on page 91.) Students will have a secure basis of understanding on which to build the numerical skills of addition, subtraction, multiplication, and division if, for example, they are able:

Addition
4. To interpret an addition fact written in symbols by putting out two sets of objects and combining them.
5. To interpret an addition fact stated in words as a movement on a number line.
6. To make up a story to fit a given addition fact in the context of shopping, using the language of price increase.

Subtration
7. To interpret a subtraction fact written in symbols by putting out a set of objects and taking some away.
8. To interpret a subtraction fact written in symbols by putting out two sets of objects and comparing them.
9. To interpret a subtraction fact stated in words as a movement on a number line.
10. To make up a story to fit a given subtraction fact in the context of shopping, using the language of comparison, e.g., "more expensive" or "less expensive."

Multiplication

11. To interpret a multiplication fact written in symbols by putting out the corresponding number of sets of objects.
12. To interpret a multiplication fact (using small numbers only) written in symbols as a number of steps along a number line.
13. To state the corresponding multiplication fact, given a rectangular array of objects.
14. To make up a story to fit a given multiplication fact in the context of shopping.

Division

15. To interpret a division fact written in symbols by sharing a set of objects into a number of equal subsets and determining how many in each subset.
16. To interpret a division fact written in symbols by sorting a set of objects into a number of subsets of a given size and determining the number of subsets.
17. To make up a story to fit a given division fact using the language of "shared between."

Number knowledge and mental arithmetic

10	10	11	12	13	14	15	16	17	18	19	20
9	9	10	11	12	13	14	15	16	17	18	19
8	8	9	10	11	12	13	14	15	16	17	18
7	7	8	9	10	11	12	13	14	15	16	17
6	6	7	8	9	10	11	12	13	14	15	16
5	5	6	7	8	9	10	11	12	13	14	15
4	4	5	6	7	8	9	10	11	12	13	14
3	3	4	5	6	7	8	9	10	11	12	13
2	2	3	4	5	6	7	8	9	10	11	12
1	1	2	3	4	5	6	7	8	9	10	11
0	0	1	2	3	4	5	6	7	8	9	10
+	0	1	2	3	4	5	6	7	8	9	10

100	100	110	120	130	140	150	160	170	180	190	200
90	90	100	110	120	130	140	150	160	170	180	190
80	80	90	100	110	120	130	140	150	160	170	180
70	70	80	90	100	110	120	130	140	150	160	170
60	60	70	80	90	100	110	120	130	140	150	160
50	50	60	70	80	90	100	110	120	130	140	150
40	40	50	60	70	80	90	100	110	120	130	140
30	30	40	50	60	70	80	90	100	110	120	130
20	20	30	40	50	60	70	80	90	100	110	120
10	10	20	30	40	50	60	70	80	90	100	110
0	0	10	20	30	40	50	60	70	80	90	100
+	0	10	20	30	40	50	60	70	80	90	100

FIGURE 6.7 *Addition facts*

The more knowledge of number facts instantly available to a person, the more he or she can cope with the numerical situations encountered in everyday life. Knowing by heart the 16 times table, for example, may not be essential for numeracy, but there are times when it is undoubtedly useful (although we do not recommend that level of skill for our students). The point we are making is that the more number knowledge we can help our students attain and have at their fingertips the better. Any and all number knowledge contributes to a person's confidence in manipulating the numbers which arise in practical problems. Even though we must be realistic when setting targets for low achievers, we put great emphasis on these students acquiring as much number knowledge as possible and being able to perform simple calculations mentally.

Students' number knowledge should include knowledge of addition facts and the corresponding subtraction facts (see Figure 6.7), and multiplication facts and the corresponding division facts (see Figure 6.8). Frequent, short mental arithmetic tests, set at an appropriate level for the students concerned, should not be ruled out. Because many low achievers have particular difficulty in retaining these number facts (see, for example, Biggs, 1985), frequent reinforcement is essential, as is an overt emphasis on the importance and value of committing these facts to memory. Many students respond very positively to the patterns they discover in the tables shown in Figures 6.7 and 6.8.

These targets center on number knowledge and mental arithmetic. Activities 6.2, 6.3, 6.4, 6.5, 6.6, 6.7, 6.8, 6.9, 6.10.

The targets here can also be seen as building on the foundation of the place-value work outlined in Chapter 4.

We propose, therefore, that it is realistic and worthwhile that low achievers up to the age of 12 years be able:

18. To recall, or to calculate mentally, all the addition facts given in Figure 6.7.

19. To recall, or to calculate mentally, all the corresponding subtraction facts arising from Figure 6.7. (For example, corresponding to "3 + 8 = 11" are the two subtraction facts: "11 – 8 = 3" and "11 – 3 = 8.")

20. To add mentally a single-digit number to any two- or three-digit number. (This is an extension of place value targets 18 and 20 given in Chapter 4; note especially examples where the units add up to more than 10, e.g., "145 + 8," "193 + 9.")

21. To subtract mentally a single-digit number from any two- or three-digit number. (This is an extension of place value targets 19 and 21 given in Chapter 4; note especially examples like "153 – 8" and "202 – 9.")

22. To recall, or to calculate mentally, all the multiplication facts given in Figure 6.8.

23. To recall, or to calculate mentally, all the corresponding division facts arising from Figure 6.8. (For example, corresponding to "4 x 8 = 32" are the two division facts: "32 ÷ 8," "32 ÷ 4.")

24. Mentally to multiply any single-digit or two-digit number by 10 or 100, and to state the corresponding division result.

10	0	10	20	30	40	50	60	70	80	90	100
9	0	9	18	27	36	45	54	63	72	81	90
8	0	8	16	24	32	40	48	56	64	72	80
7	0	7	14	21	28	35	42	49	56	63	70
6	0	6	12	18	24	30	36	42	48	54	60
5	0	5	10	15	20	25	30	35	40	45	50
4	0	4	8	12	16	20	24	28	32	36	40
3	0	3	6	9	12	15	18	21	24	27	30
2	0	2	4	6	8	10	12	14	16	18	20
1	0	1	2	3	4	5	6	7	8	9	10
0	0	0	0	0	0	0	0	0	0	0	0
x	0	1	2	3	4	5	6	7	8	9	10

FIGURE **6.8** *Multiplication facts*

Calculation skills

Calculators, informal methods, and algorithms

In this section we outline a realistic and useful set of calculation skills for low achievers up to the age of 12 years. This set of targets is fairly limited since in practice most calculations are carried out nowadays by electronic machines. Because of this, our primary target is for students to know what calculations to enter on a calculator in order to solve problems across the range of different situations encountered in everyday life. This must be more important than the students' facility with pencil and paper calculations. Furthermore, when doing calculations without a calculator (stressed earlier in Chapter 2), the students must be allowed to use informal methods if they wish, instead of the formal algorithms of arithmetic. Some students need the security of an algorithm but, in our experience, many are more competent in dealing with calculations when encouraged to use whatever methods make sense to them. Informal methods are always based upon the individual's own repertoire of number knowledge and make use of relationships with which they are familiar and confident. Often they are related to the student's experience of handling money.

Sean, aged 11, was taking part in a game called Shopkeeper (see Activity 8.7). He needed to work out the total cost of 5 articles at 12¢ each. In his head, talking out loud, he reasoned: "Five tens, that's 50¢, and five twos, that's ten. That's 60¢." His next problem was to work out the cost of 5 articles at 17¢ each. He started off in the same way, found that the problem was too complex, turned to his calculator, and entered "5 x 17 =."

This appears to illustrate the right balance we should aim for in our work with low achievers. First, encourage them to use their own methods that make sense to them: it really would not help Sean to teach him to set out his calculation for "5 x 17" in the conventional way. Second, allow them to turn to a calculator when their informal methods fail them: Sean showed good mathematical thinking by recognizing the need for multiplication and being able to interpret the answer produced by the calculator.

Consequently, in the following targets we have not specified that students should learn one particular algorithm for any operation. As noted before, these skills are pointless on their own without the ability to connect them to real situations, to the manipulation of concrete materials, and to the corresponding language. We have therefore included the

Targets for calculation skills. See Activity 6.18. Activities from Chapters 4 and 8 would also be appropriate for these targets.

phrase "arising in a practical situation" in each target below. Often the structure of the practical situation prompts a student to develop an informal method of solving the problem.

We would be satisfied if many of our low achievers, by the age of 12 years and using informal methods (written or mental or a combination of the two) or a standard algorithm, were able:

25. To perform an addition of two numbers with up to three digits, arising in a practical situation.

26. To perform a subtraction with numbers up to three digits, arising in a practical situation.

27. To perform a multiplication of a two-digit number by a single-digit number, arising in a practical situation.

28. To perform a division of a two-digit number by a single-digit number, arising in a practical situation (and including examples with a remainder).

An illustration will clarify Target 28 and also reinforce the importance of our accepting informal methods for calculations. During a shopping project, Claire (aged 10 years) had collected data about prices for packages of chocolate cookies. One package of 5 cookies cost 66¢. She realized that she had to find "66 ÷ 5" to work out the cost per cookie. Not knowing an algorithm, she jotted down a jumble of figures, and came up with the answer. She explained how she worked it out:

"If they were 10¢ each, it would be 50¢ ... another 2¢ makes 10 ... 60¢ ... another 1¢, that's 5¢, so 65¢. So it's 10, 12, 13¢ . . . 13¢ and a little bit."

This process is certainly good enough for us to count as successful for Target 28!

The two best ways we see to help our students achieve the above targets are: (1) to provide them with plenty of experience of shopping situations, using dimes and pennies to solve problems practically; and (2) to engage in much more explicit discussion and validation of informal methods, such as that shown above, which arise naturally from the manipulation of the coins.

Handling big numbers

Using calculators, students can explore problems with big numbers, which would otherwise be inaccessible to them. We find that students become highly motivated when allowed to handle big number problems.

Consequently, we include as important targets that the students should be able:

29. To say in words the name of any whole number produced as an answer on a calculator (in other words, to interpret numbers up to 99 999 999, i.e., ninety-nine million, nine hundred ninety-nine thousand, nine hundred ninety-nine.)

Targets for handling big numbers. Activities 6.14, 6.15, 6.16, 6.17, and 6.18.

30. To enter on a calculator any number given in words, with up to eight digits.

31. To compare two numbers with up to eight digits and determine which is the greater and which the lesser.

Suggested activities

Having identified the importance of giving low achievers a secure understanding of their work with numbers, you will want to give them activities designed to develop the connections between symbols, language, pictorial and concrete representations, and real-life situations. One of the best ways of getting insights into students understanding of number operations is to have them make up stories to go with results. This idea is incorporated into the following activities.

Numerous simple number games (both small-group and whole-class activities) can be used effectively to develop number knowledge and ability in simple mental arithmetic. We provide just a few examples of games we have found to be successful in helping students with Targets 18–24. For further ideas see ILEA (1985) and Duncan (1978).

Activity 6.1 Number Operations

Materials

A sheet of "results" using addition, subtraction, multiplication, and division, as appropriate, using numbers up to 20 (e.g. 3 + 8, 14 − 6, 12 x 3, 4 ÷ 2, etc.); a calculator; a supply of number lines (marked from 0 to 20); supplies of linked cubes and play money coins; blank paper or a cassette recorder.

> Develop connections between the symbols of number operations and language, pictures, concrete materials, and real situations. Targets 4–17.

Method

Divide the students into several small groups. For each calculation on the sheet, each group must:

(i) enter the calculation on the calculator
(ii) work out how to show it on the number line
(iii) decide how to show it with linked cubes
(iv) make up a problem with the coins
(v) write a story which corresponds to the calculation (or record one on the cassette recorder if they have difficulty with writing).

For example, given "14 − 6," they could:

(i) enter this on the calculator to get the result "8"
(ii) count back on a number line 6 steps from 14
(iii) put out a row of 14 linked cubes and another row of 6, and compare them to find the difference
(iv) make up a problem where someone with 14¢ spends 6¢, showing this with the coins
(v) write this story: "Bill is 14 and his brother Ben is 6. How much older is Bill?"

The group may divide up the work however they like, individually, in pairs, or as a whole group. If they decide to work in small units, they must check each other's work for accuracy. This helps to create a situation where they all feel responsible for the group's complete assignment.

When they have decided on the various responses, the group calls the teacher over to demonstrate their connections. If some students are having difficulty making the connections, you could give various prompts, e.g., "use a story about ages."

Variations

Instead of starting with a calculation, the teacher can give a number line diagram or a story as a starting point.

Development of knowledge of number facts. Targets 18, 19, and 22.

Activity 6.2 Four in a Line

0	18	4	14	13	16	2	1
3	14	7	12	11	6	13	17
15	6	9	10	8	10	9	5
12	11	8	11	10	9	7	15
16	14	9	10	9	6	13	16
5	7	10	8	10	8	11	4
18	12	6	11	12	7	13	3
19	2	4	15	4	5	17	20

(a) Addition

20	14	9	18	13	15	10	19
11	7	2	3	6	3	7	8
16	5	0	4	2	0	5	11
12	3	1	6	3	1	2	17
15	6	4	0	2	4	6	10
9	5	0	2	3	0	1	16
8	7	1	4	1	5	7	13
19	10	14	12	17	9	8	18

(b) Subtraction

1	7	45	56	60	35	21	5
81	100	8	6	12	20	9	25
27	4	18	40	24	18	8	54
50	12	10	20	10	30	6	90
63	16	24	36	12	40	16	48
70	40	20	30	10	18	36	32
64	9	8	24	6	30	4	49
2	14	28	42	72	80	15	3

(c) Multiplication

FIGURE 6.9 *Boards for four in a line (for Activity 6.2)*

Materials

A board laid out as in Figure 6.9(a); either Packs A and B of cards (from activities in Chapter 4) with extra cards for "10" included, or some other means to generate numbers from 0 to 10; a set of counters for each player in different colors.

Method

In turn, players turn over a card from each pack. Then they place one of their colored counters on a square containing the sum of the two numbers revealed, if one is available. The players should have enough counters so they can use them for finding the sums, especially in the early stages of learning these addition facts. The first player to get four counters in a line (across, down, or diagonally) is the winner. (The arrangements of numbers on the boards in Figure 6.9 take into account the expected frequency of various answers.)

Variations

(i) Adapt the board and the packs of cards so that students can practice adding multiples of 10. Simply replace each number on the cards and on the board by the same number multiplied by 10.

(ii) For subtraction, use sets of cards labeled up to 20 and the board layout shown in Figure 6.9(b). Students have to find the difference between the two numbers displayed, thus focusing on Target 19.

(iii) For multiplication practice (Target 22), use the board layout shown in Figure 6.9(c). In the early stages (and later for some), allow students to use calculators or copies of Figure 6.8 for the multiplication version.

Activity 6.3 One to Twenty

Materials

Packs A and B with tens, elevens, and twelves added, or some other means, such as dodecahedron (twelve-faced) dice, for generating numbers from 1 to 12; a card (30 cm by 5 cm) for each player, marked off in twenty squares and numbered sequentially from 1 to 20 (see Figure 6.10); 20 counters for each player to place in the squares and cover the numbers; possibly a calculator for working out the final scores.

Strengthening knowledge of addition facts. Target 18.

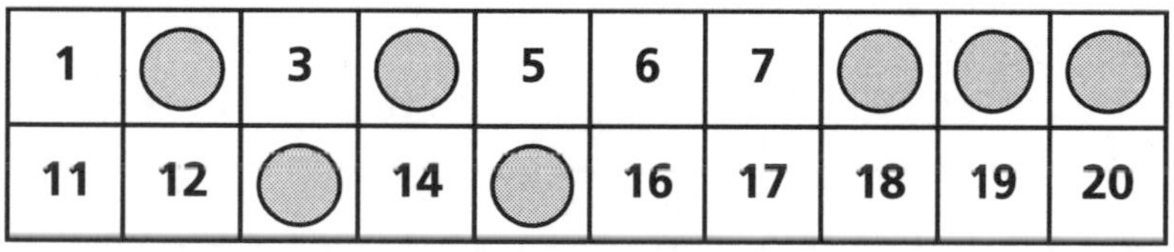

FIGURE **6.10** *One-to-twenty game (for Activity 6.3)*

Method

The object of the game is to finish with the smallest score against you by covering up the numbers on your strip. In turn, players are dealt two cards by the referee, one each from Packs A and B. They work out the sum of the two numbers revealed. The players then use their counters to cover over this total or any combination of numbers which add up to it. The referee checks that this has been done correctly. At any stage of the game a player may decide to be dealt just one card rather than two.

Any player who cannot make up the total given by his or her cards is out. When all players are out, they add up the numbers not covered on their card (some may need to use a calculator here). The sum counts against them.

In Figure 6.10, if the player is dealt "8" and "5," giving a total of 13, he or she may choose to put counters on 7, 5, and 1; on 12 and 1; or on 7 and 6. If "1" and "1" are dealt giving a total of 2, he or she is out since numbers totaling 2 no longer remain on the strip.

Variations

For a simplified version, use a strip numbered up to 10 and conventional six-faced dice. Just score the number of squares not covered.

Activity 6.4 Addition and Multiplication Tables

Practice of the addition and multiplication facts in Figures 6.7 and 6.8. Targets 18 and 22.

Materials

A calculator and a blank 11 by 11 grid for each student.

Method

From time to time students should make their own copies of Figures 6.7 and 6.8, using a calculator to help them fill in the numbers where necessary. Engage them in explicit discussion of the patterns they observe as they do this. Each pattern they observe helps students make sense of the way the numbers are arranged in the table.

Occasionally chanting the multiplication tables as a means of memorizing these facts can be very effective (especially for those students whose preferred learning mode is auditory or musical). We emphasize again that students need many experiences with numbers that help them understand, not just memorize. If doing this with a group of children, one useful tip is to get them to say each result twice, for example, "one three is three, one three is three, two threes are six, two threes are six, etc." The value of this approach is that the children who do not get a result the first time actually say it correctly the second time.

When students record their successes they affirm their own learning while focusing their attention on the more difficult facts.

If you give regular short tests of these number facts, students can use a copy of each table as a record sheet. The first time they get a particular result correct they circle it on their copy. The second time, they color in the square completely, obliterating the number, since they now know this result and do not need to look it up! Each student aims to get the whole table colored in eventually. You can also use the students' record sheets to show which number facts need special attention.

For example, with one class of 11- and 12-year-olds, Derek discovered that no one had yet circled the result for "7 x 8." So he made this a special target. In fact, nearly all the students learned this one once he made a fuss about it and pointed out the following pattern, based on the sequence of digits: 1, 2, 3, 4, 5, 6, 7, 8:

$12 = 3 \times 4$

$56 = 7 \times 8$

Activity 6.5 Turning the Tables

Understanding the corresponding addition and subtraction facts (Target 19), and multiplication and division facts (Target 23); strengthening the connections between symbols, language, and real situations.

Method

This class activity can be used regularly and frequently to usefully fill up the odd five minutes at the start or end of a lesson. Write one addition fact (taken from Figure 6.7) on the board, for example: "40 + 70 = 110." Then challenge the class, asking the students as many questions you can derive from this fact as possible. A few are listed below:

What are 40 and 70?

What are 70 and 40?

What is the total cost of a pen at 70¢ and a pencil at 40¢?

What is the difference between 110 and 70?

If I am 70 years old, how many years until I am 110 years old?

How much is left from $1.10 if I spend 40¢?

After some experience of doing this, some students may make up their own questions on short notice, especially if key words or phrases (add, subtract, take away, total cost, older, younger, difference between, etc.) are written on the board and have been used frequently in meaningful situations.

The same activity can be used with a multiplication fact. With "7 x 8 = 56," you could ask questions such as:

What is 7 multiplied by 8?

How many eights in 56?

What is 56 divided by 8?

What is 56 divided by 7?

How much would you pay for 8 apples at 7¢ each?

Share 56 marbles between 8 children: how many each?

My car does 8 km per L: how far can I drive with 7 L?

Activity 6.6 Tables Jigsaw

Materials

A copy of any one of the tables in Figures 6.7 and 6.8 for each child.

Method

Along the lines of the grid, each student cuts the table up into a number of pieces to make a jigsaw puzzle. Students exchange their puzzles and must reassemble the table. Simple, but effective!

> Understanding the patterns in Figures 6.7 and 6.8, as an aid to learning addition and multiplication facts. Targets 18 and 22.

Activity 6.7 What Did I Do?

Materials

One calculator for each pair of students.

Method

A two-digit number is chosen, written down prominently, and entered on the calculator by one of a pair of students. That student then presses either + or − followed by a single digit, then hands the calculator to the other student and asks, "What did I do?" The second student must get the starting number back on the display, again by pressing either + or − followed by a single digit. For example, if the starting number is 58 and one student presses "+ 7" to have 65 displayed, the other student must press "− 7" to get back to 58.

> Practice in adding a single-digit number to a two- or three-digit number (Target 20) and subtracting a single-digit number from a two- or three-digit number (Target 21).

We suggest that the starting number is changed after each student has had five turns. Once students are confident with two-digit numbers, the game can be played using a three-digit number on the display. It is useful to have a third student act as referee in this game.

Variations

Students can play the same basic game focusing on Target 24. The first student can choose to multiply by 10 or 100 or just add or subtract a single digit as before. If he or she chooses a multiplication, the other student must undo this by dividing by 10 or 100.

Students may want to keep score or just play the game for its own sake.

Activity 6.8 More Grids

Method

Extend Activity 4.10 in Chapter 4 by using instructions for addition and subtraction of any single-digit number along the axes of the grids. For example, with a starting number of 378 in the top left corner of the grid, the instructions ADD 3 and SUBTRACT 8 would lead to a finishing number of 358 in the bottom right corner.

Further practice in adding a single-digit number to a two- or three-digit number (Target 20) and subtracting a single-digit number from a two- or three-digit number (Target 21).

Activity 6.9 I Have, Who Has?

Materials

Prepare a set of 25 cards with multiplication questions on one side. The answer to one question is written on the back of the card with the next question. The answer to the question on the last card in the set is written on the reverse of the first card. No answers should be repeated. Figure 6.11 shows a set of cards designed for practicing multiplication facts up to 6 x 6 and the 10 times table. Note that this arrangement makes a cycle of questions and answers, allowing any card to be the starting card in the game described below.

Practicing recall of multiplication facts. Target 22.

Method

The cards are shuffled and dealt out to the players. The last card is placed in the center of the table, question uppermost. If, for example, this is "5 x 3," the dealer says, "Who has five times three?" Whoever has the card with "15" on the reverse then places it next to the question card, saying, "I have 15." When all agree this is correct, that player turns the card over, on top of the first card, to reveal the next question. He or she says, "Who has six times four?" Play proceeds like this, the object being to get rid of all the cards in your hand.

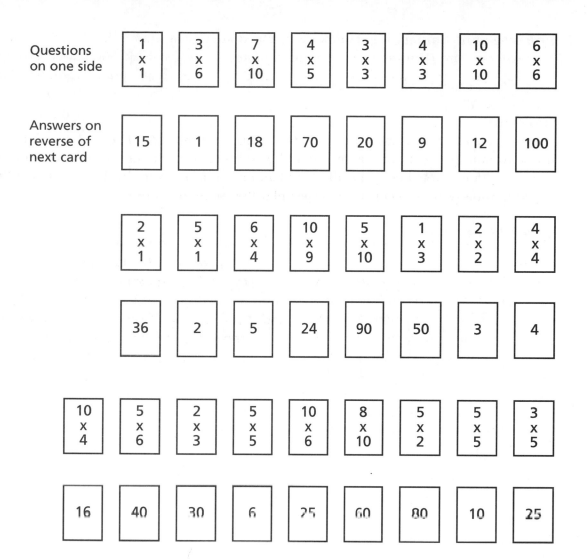

Questions on one side

| 1 x 1 | 3 x 6 | 7 x 10 | 4 x 5 | 3 x 3 | 4 x 3 | 10 x 10 | 6 x 6 |

Answers on reverse of next card

| 15 | 1 | 18 | 70 | 20 | 9 | 12 | 100 |

| 2 x 1 | 5 x 1 | 6 x 4 | 10 x 9 | 5 x 10 | 1 x 3 | 2 x 2 | 4 x 4 |

| 36 | 2 | 5 | 24 | 90 | 50 | 3 | 4 |

| 10 x 4 | 5 x 6 | 2 x 3 | 5 x 5 | 10 x 6 | 8 x 10 | 5 x 2 | 5 x 5 | 3 x 5 |

| 16 | 40 | 30 | 6 | 25 | 60 | 80 | 10 | 25 |

FIGURE 6.11 *I Have, Who Has? cards for multiplication facts (for Activity 6.9)*

Variations

(i) Play the game in reverse, starting with the "answers." For example, "Who has 15?" is followed by "I have 5 x 3."

(ii) Play this as a class game. Distribute one card to each member of the class. One person starts, calling out their question. Whoever has the answer calls this out, turns over his or her card and calls out the next question. One student times the class with a stopwatch to determine how long it takes to get back to the starting card. Display a graphical record to show the class times over a number of days, and challenge them to beat their own record.

(iii) Use addition facts cards instead.

Activity 6.10 Board Games

Materials

A board layout such as the one shown in Figure 6.12; counters and dice.

Practice of any aspect of mental arithmetic and number sense. Target 20.

48	46	44	43	38	35	34	32
50							30
55		91	90	87	84		29
57		93			83		24
59		99	Finish 100		80		22
60					79		21
65	66	68	70	73	76		19
							15
Start	1	2	4	5	8	10	12

FIGURE **6.12** *A simple board game (for Activity 6.10)*

Method

Figure 6.12 shows the layout for a simple board game designed to give a small group of students the opportunity to practice adding a single-digit number (up to 6) to a two-digit number. In turn, each player throws a die and moves his or her counter the number of places shown on the die. The player then adds the number on the die to the number on the square landed on. If the answer is larger than the number on the next square, the player moves forward one more square; if it is smaller he or she moves back one square; if it is the same he or she stays put. The game is simply a race from start to finish. If you (or the students) want, you can use a common rule for such board games about finishing exactly at the end.

When designing board games like this, keep the rules simple so that once one group of students has played the game, one of them can be responsible for explaining it to the next group.

Variations

Provide pairs of students with appropriate materials, such as a sheet of cardstock, 2 cm squared paper, scissors, glue, coloring pens, a calculator, counters, and dice. Ask them to invent their own board game to practice a set of appropriate number skills. You could specify that the game must involve multiplying pairs of numbers from the table in Figure 6.8.

> Students often need drill and routine practice in order to master the basic facts. Drill and practice do not have to be dull and pointless.

Activity 6.11 Computer Drill and Practice Programs

A wide range of computer software is available for drill and practice. The student is given a series of questions for practicing some particular skill, such as addition of two numbers. A common option is to vary the level of difficulty: a computer can, of course, go on and on generating questions at random within a given range. The program gives the student some kind of reward for a correct response, usually an audiovisual display on the computer monitor. This type of software can be very effective. However, be wary of any software where the computer's response to an incorrect answer is actually more fun than that for a correct one!

> The combination of computer-assisted instruction (CAI) and positive reinforcement from the teacher is significantly more effective for low achievers than CAI on its own (Moore, 1988).

An obvious benefit in using a computer to generate questions, record, correct, and reward students' responses is that the activity does not demand much from the teacher. However, make time to supplement the computer's rewards with rewards of your own, such as praise, encouragement, and time.

Activity 6.12 Picture Puzzles

Dot-to-dot puzzles are a familiar and simple technique for rewarding students for doing a series of arithmetic exercises. Place a sheet of tracing paper over an outline drawing of some familiar object and mark significant points in the outline with dots. Make up a set of exercises, each with a different answer. Write the answers to the exercises in the correct sequence next to the dots. Add a few more dots and distractor answers. The puzzle and the set of exercises can be photocopied for distribution to the class. Students answer the questions and join up the corresponding dots to make the picture. The gradual emergence of the picture constitutes the reward for success.

A variation is to make a puzzle in which the picture and the background are divided up into several regions. Write the answers to the exercises in the regions within the picture and put some distractor answers in the background regions. The picture emerges as the students shade in the regions containing the answers to the exercises. Figure 6.13 shows an example of each type of picture puzzle.

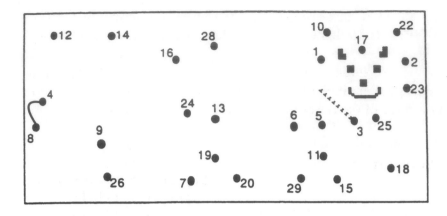

2+2 4+5 9+7 20+8 1+0 4+6 10+7 10+12 1+1 20+3 20+5 2+1
3+2 5+6 6+9 9+20 1+5 10+3 9+10 10+10 4+3 20+4 6+20 5+3

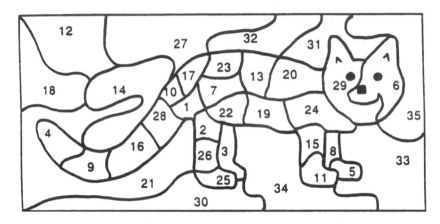

FIGURE 6.13 *Picture puzzles (for Activity 6.12)*

You may not have time to prepare many puzzles. However, the students themselves, once they have the idea, can prepare their own puzzles to give to each other to solve. You could ask them to make a picture puzzle for practicing subtraction with two-digit numbers. They could use the calculator while preparing the series of exercises, to ensure that they put the correct answers on the drawing.

Activity 6.13 Calculator Marking

Allow students to use calculators to mark their own or a partner's answers. This simple technique enables them to practice any calculation skill, such as those in Targets 25-28. An enjoyable way of providing the arithmetic exercises is to use packs of cards (e.g., Packs A and B) or some other means of generating numbers at random.

For example, imagine that two students are practicing subtraction with two two-digit numbers (Target 26). Each student "deals" the other two two-digit numbers. They then work out their answer subtracting the smaller number from the larger without the calculator, using whatever method they wish. The fun of this is that sometimes one student is dealt an easy question and the other a hard one, or vice versa. They then use the calculator to check each other's answers. Points are scored for correct answers.

If the students are using a pack of cards to generate the questions, reward success by having the student retain the cards. In this way the game has a natural ending: when the supply of cards runs out.

Clearly, this is an activity for two students at about the same level of arithmetic skill. It is a more effective way to engage them in routine practice of operations than the conventional approach of giving a page of exercises and having the teacher mark the answers some time later.

Activity 6.14 Big Number Problems

Method

Students often enjoy tackling really big problems with their calculators. Some are given below, all of which need some preliminary discussion about the variables involved.

> Tackling big number problems using a calculator (Target 29) and comparing answers with other students (Target 31).

> How many minutes have you lived (approximately)?
> How much milk (ice cream, pencils, etc.) could you buy with a thousand (hundred thousand, million) dollars?
> How many seconds do you spend in bed in a week?
> If you earn $5 an hour every hour, how much will you earn in a lifetime?
> About how many letters are there in a book?

For this last problem, groups of students could each choose a book and the class could compare them. Calculate the number of letters approximately by multiplying the number of pages by the number of lines per page, and then by the approximate number of letters per line. This would be an excellent opportunity to explore the nature of estimation.

Activity 6.15 Big Number Challenges

Method

Give the students a set of cards representing a selection of keys on the calculator. You can vary the level of difficulty with the cards used. Always include one card with an "equals sign". The

> Exploring big numbers. Targets 29–31.

challenge is to arrange all the cards into a key sequence on the calculator, aiming to get the largest possible answer. Several students should work individually on the problem, comparing their largest answers so far at each stage. Have them say the numbers out loud.

Figure 6.14 shows an example of a set of these cards, and one student's suggestion for arranging them, producing the answer "seventy-nine thousand forty-eight." (Is this, in fact, the biggest possible answer?)

The note about "order of operations" at the end of Activity 4.12 also applies here.

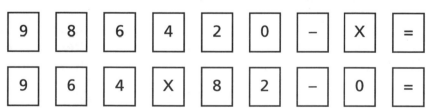

FIGURE 6.14 *Example of cards for use with Activity 6.15*

Activity 6.16 Lesser-Known Facts of the Universe

This set of worksheets has proved very popular with all students who enjoy exploring the absurd suggestions contained in them. For further ideas about encouraging low achievers to investigate amazing facts, see Womack (1988) or any world almanac or record book.

Practical measurement, relationships between units, a big number given in words, a calculation using a calculator, and a large number at the end to be interpreted. Targets from Chapter 4 and Targets 29 and 30.

Lesser-known fact no. 1:

HAMSTERS AND ELEPHANTS.

Use a scale to weigh a hamster. Write the answer in kg (for example, 125 g = 0.125 kg). A hamster's weight is __ kg. An adult male African elephant weighs about 5 000 kilograms. About how many hamsters would be needed to balance this elephant?

Animal	Weight of Animal in kg	Weight of Animal in Hamsters

Lesser-known fact no. 2: END-TO-END CHILDREN.

Measure your height in centimeters. Change this to meters (for example, 135 cm = 1.35 m) My height is __ m. It's about 85 000 m from Vancouver, BC to Bellingham, WA. About how many children of your size could fit end-to-end along the road from Vancouver to Bellingham?

Distance	Length of Child	Total Distance in Children = Lengths

Lesser-known fact no. 3: SWALLOWING A SWIMMING POOL.

Use a large measuring jug to find out how much water you or a friend can drink at one time. Write the answer in L (for example, 850 mL = 0.850 L, 1500 mL = 1.500 L). I can drink __ L of water at a time. About how many children would be needed to drink a swimming pool which holds 450 000 L of water?

Container	Volume of Container	Liters per Child	Children Required to Drink Volume

Activity 6.17 The E-game

This activity helps students understand the process of making an estimate and learning that the first digit and the number of digits in each number are the most significant factors in determining the size of the estimate.

Building confidence in handling big numbers and experience with the front-end technique of estimation. Targets 29–31.

Materials

A die and one calculator that displays an "E" (for ERROR) if asked to produce an answer with more than eight digits.

Method

The die is rolled and the number on the die becomes the "target digit," which is entered on the calculator. Players then take turns adding numbers to the number on display. The number entered must have the same number of digits as the current display. A point is scored each time a player gets the target digit as the first digit in the answer. The round ends when an E is displayed, and the player who produces the E loses a point. The students can discover several interesting strategies for playing this game.

Example: The die is rolled and the target digit is "3." This is entered on the calculator. A and B then might play as follows:

PLAYER	ENTRY	DISPLAY	SCORE
A	+ 5	= 8	0
B	+ 9	= 17	0
A	+ 20	= 37	1
B	+ 62	= 99	0
A	+ 99	= 198	0
B	+ 150	= 348	1

etc.

Variation

The E-game can also be played using multiplication rather than addition. The rules are the same except that only single-digit numbers (greater than 1) may be entered each time. For example, with "3" as the target digit, a game might proceed like this:

PLAYER	ENTRY	DISPLAY	SCORE
A	x 5	= 15	0
B	x 2	= 30	1
A	x 9	= 270	0
B	x 4	= 1080	0
A	x 3	= 3240	1
B	x 9	= 29160	0

A	x 4	= 116640	0
B	x 3	= 349920	1
A	x 9	= 3149280	1
B	x 9	= 28343520	0
A	x 2	= 56687040	0
B	x 2	= E	-1

Activity 6.18 Where Did I Come From?

This activity has been adapted from an article by Lappan & Winter (1978).

Materials

One calculator for each pair or small group of students; "Where Did I Come From?" game cards; writing tools.

This activity provides interesting practice with numbers of any difficulty range for either multiplication or addition. Targets 25–31 depending on teacher design.

Method

This game is a variation on BINGO. The teacher constructs a game card with an appropriate number of squares (your decision). In each square is a product and all the factors of each product used for that card are found at the bottom of the card (See Figure 6.15). In turn, students (working alone or with partners) must then select two factors, multiply them with the calculator, locate the appropriate product, and write the factors in the square with the product. The object of the game is to make a line or fill out the card completely.

77	275	200	1075	60	110
860	341	50	165	473	105
430	217	215	500	70	140
1333	220	150	301	155	775

5	7	10	11	12	15	20
		25	31	43		

FIGURE 6.15 *Example game card for use with Activity 6.18*

Variations

 (i) Sums and their addends could be used instead of products.
 (ii) The level of difficulty and the number of squares can be increased or reduced depending on the learners. For example, use a limited amount of very big numbers.

(iii) Encourage students to try different strategies to find their BINGO:
  - estimate the factors by comparing products
  - identify even and odd numbers to help select factors
  - use division (or subtraction) to find the factors thus eliminating guess work.
(iv) Ask students extension and enrichment questions based on factors and products such as, "Could you use other factors to generate these products?" "What might they be?" "How did you figure it out?"

Activity 6.19 Have Calculator, Will Solve

This activity is especially good for learning important words and language patterns. Students can do just ten of these sentences each day at the start of their lesson over a few weeks. This provides practice for Targets 1–3.

Materials
Large sheet of cardstock or bristol board
Packs of cards with various appropriate numbers written on them.
One calculator per group of students.

Method
Write on a large sheet of bristol board a standard sentence incorporating one of the structures, leaving blank boxes for the numbers involved. The boxes should be about the size of a calculator. The following are examples of sentences from various classes of problems, which the reader (not the students) should now be able to identify using Figures 6.1 and 6.5:
  - If a price of __ is increased by __, the new price is __.
  - The cost of __ m of cotton fabric at __ per m is __.
  - $__ shared between __ is $__ each.

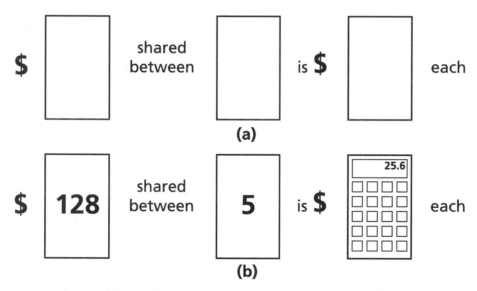

FIGURE 6.16 *Calculator sentences for equal sharing (Activity 6.19)*

Packs of cards with an appropriate number written on each are placed face down in two of the boxes. Students (preferably working in pairs) turn over one card from each pack. They then enter the appropriate calculation onto their calculator and place the calculator, with the answer on display, in the remaining empty box to complete the sentence. Figure 6.16(a) shows the layout for a sentence using the relationship of division as equal sharing (money ÷ sets). In Figure 6.16(b), the students have turned over cards to display the numbers "128" and "5," have entered "128 ÷ 5 =" on the calculator, and placed the calculator in the final box to complete the sentence.

When focusing on the language of subtraction as comparing, incorporate another blank box in the sentence. In this box, place a card that reads "more than" on one side and "less than" on the other, or the corresponding language for each context (e.g., "longer than" and "shorter than," "heavier than" and "lighter than").

Sentences such as these use important language patterns:

- __ is __ (more than/less than) __
- $__ is $__ (more expensive than/less expensive than) $__
- __ miles is __ miles (further than/nearer than) __ miles
- __ grams is __ grams (heavier than/lighter than) __ grams

Figure 6.17(a) shows the layout for one such example in the context of length. In Figure 6.17(b), the students turned over cards showing the numbers 28 and 59, decided that 28 m is less than 59 m, and set the card in the third box to display "shorter than." Then they entered "59 – 28 =" on their calculators and placed the calculator in the remaining box to complete the sentence.

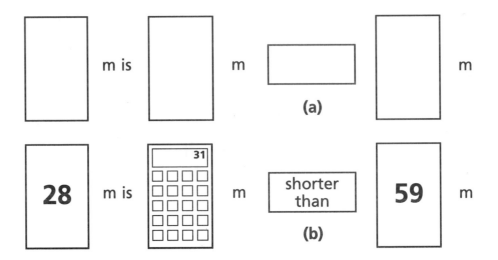

FIGURE 6.17 *Calculator sentences for comparison of length (for Activity 6.19)*

Variations

Students can copy the completed sentence into their books for reinforcement, record keeping, and future reference. They could also provide an estimate before using the calculator.

When doing subtraction sentences, students often enter the numbers in the wrong order in the early stages. When they do this their calculator display shows the answer to the question but with a minus sign (e.g. "28 – 59 =" gives "–31"). We simply say that when the calculator displays the minus sign, they have put the smaller number in first and subtracted the larger number. When this happens, they should do it again the right way round and make sure they get an answer without the minus sign. If some students appear ready to deal with negative numbers, tell them about owing money or below zero temperatures as familiar contexts for understanding.

Computer activities

If you have access to computers, you may want to supplement your instruction with interactive computer programs. Have students work in pairs through the activities in many of the high quality products available on the market. We refer the reader to journals which review educational computer software. Relying on vicarious and artificial relevance, these can provide excellent practice. However, these programs must never replace meaningful, purposeful activities which have immediate and genuine relevance for the students (refer to Chapter 2).

Estimation activities

Estimation activities can help to develop a sense of number, a key component of numeracy skills. We want to give our students experience in estimating so they are able to make reasonable estimates. Learning targets center on two types of estimates: estimating quantities and complex computations. To estimate quantities, compare unknown quantities with a known quantity, partition them into known quantities, or use mental computation (as if estimating measurement). Strategies for estimating computations have been outlined earlier in this chapter.

Estimating quantities

Chapter 5 suggests several activities to engage students in the estimation of length, weight, capacity, and time. In this chapter, we include ideas for estimating quantities in sets of objects.

Activity 6.20 Reference Items for Sets

Compare unknown sets to known amounts. Target 3.

Materials

Unifix cubes, candies, stacks of trading cards, etc. This list is limited only by what is relevant to the lives of the students and your imagination.

Method

Show a set of 19 unifix cubes connected in a straight row and ask the students to estimate (guess) the number of cubes in the formation. Do not allow time to count. Then show a set of 15 cubes and tell the students the number of cubes. Ask again how many they now think are in the row of 19 cubes. Remove the 15 cubes and leave the 19 cubes in view. Ask if this row has more or less than the 15-cube row and how many more or less. Then show the two rows together again and question students about how they decided on their revised estimates.

Variations

Use different numbers of cubes in other formations. Use other materials as well.

One unique variation is to fill a clear jar or other container with only two colors of jelly beans or other candies. Ask the students to estimate the number of one of the colors. When they have done that, tell them how many there are of the other color and have them revise their estimates. Repeat with different-sized jars and types of candy over several days to provide enough practice for students to become confident with the numbers in the sets in question.

Activity 6.21 Estimating by Partitioning

Materials

A jar or clear container of pennies or other small collectibles interesting to students.

Involve students in counting out the groups. Target 3.

Method

Show a jar of 400 or 500 pennies. Ask for estimates from the students. Then count out 50 pennies from the jar and ask for revised estimates of the total number of pennies (not just those remaining). Count out another 50 pennies and have students revise their estimates again. Provide guidance by suggesting that they compare the amount remaining with that counted out. Repeat this activity with different-sized jars and types of materials over the course of several days to provide enough practice for students to become confident and proficient.

Estimating calculations

The following activities are suitable for addition questions. Query the students about the appropriateness of their answers: "Does your answer make sense given the numbers and the situation?" To respond to this inquiry students will need to estimate the answer or answers.

Activity 6.22 Practicing Estimation

Do this activity in the context of understanding the purpose of estimation. Do preliminary work with estimation first. Target 3.

Materials

Calculator, paper, pencil

Method

When students are producing estimates, encourage them to use whatever method of computation they feel is best: paper and pencil, the calculator, or mental computation.

Keeping in mind that we want our students to be able to check the results of their computations with a quick estimate, give them situations in which the computation has already been completed. The question then becomes, "Is this answer close to the correct answer?" Students then check using an estimate, employing a method suggested by the teacher or selecting one of their choice. Question the students about their estimates (how they did it and why they did it in a particular way) and if they think the answer given is reasonable. Students may want to compute the complex questions on the calculator to check their estimates.

Variations

This activity can be done in small groups with students working together to find appropriate estimates. Students can compare estimates for speed and accuracy and complete the original question as well.

Activity 6.23 gives meaningful practice with estimation strategies for one of the most common uses of estimation in real life. Target 3.

Activity 6.23 Do I Have Enough?

The motivation for completing this activity is the utility of the exercise, the desire to learn, and the enjoyment of working with other students.

Materials

Activity cards or sheets for each group of students; calculators

Method

Give students a list or pictures of consumer items (as in Figure 6.18) from which to choose a specified number of items to "purchase." Ask if the amount of money printed at the top is enough to "purchase" what they want, not enough, or too close to decide by estimating (thus making an exact computation necessary). The students make their estimates and then exchange answers. They can also find the exact amount using their calculators or other method. If there is a difference of opinion regarding the estimate or exact answer, students should call the teacher to settle the matter. Ensure that the students understand that the model solutions are examples and other ways of making the estimates are correct as long as they are relatively quick and accurate and can help determine the reasonableness of the calculator display.

Variations

Try this game as a whole class using an overhead transparency. This would give the students experience with the process of the activity before attempting it in small groups.

I have $100.00

FIGURE 6.18 *Sample activity card for Do I Have Enough? (Activity 6.23)*

Key teaching points

- When first teaching operations, use contexts and situations that generate more purposeful, relevant, genuine, and practical problems; those which are familiar to students such as money and sets of things.
- Begin with concrete representations of the operations and then move to calculations.
- Consider introducing the equal-sharing relationship of division before the relationships of multiplication.
- Allow time for students to think about what the operations mean; help them to verbalize their new understandings.
- Allow students to rely on the calculator for complex calculations so they can focus on the structure of the problems.
- Teach estimation skills to help students determine the reasonableness of a calculation and solidify their conceptual understanding of the operations.

QUESTIONS FOR DISCUSSION WITH COLLEAGUES

1. Are there other important numeracy targets in addition to the ones considered in this chapter? What might those be?

2. For the various classes of problems described in this chapter, brainstorm other examples which are practical, genuine, and purposeful for your students.

3. Do you agree with our suggested priorities for establishing the different relationships of the operations? How might you teach them and why would you use that method?

4. How can you best help a student to internalize a mathematical structure which they have discovered through using a calculator in the fuzzy zone of a series of examples? How might concrete materials or estimating be helpful?

5. How do *you* actually calculate the answers to various arithmetical problems, such as finding the cost of 25 articles at 24¢ each? What is the best balance between the use of calculators, algorithms, and informal methods? Do those who use informal methods all do the questions the same way?

6. What is your view on the issue of encouraging the use of informal methods as opposed to teaching traditional algorithms?

7
Common
Fractions

Important characteristics of fractions

Both common fractions and decimals will always be part of our everyday lives and must therefore be included in any program for low achievers. Knowledge of fractions is necessary not only to progress in higher mathematics and science. It is required in everyday conversations, when understanding and communicating about parts of whole regions or sets, some measurements, money transactions, and decimals.

> Knowing how to deal with fractions, part of our everyday world, is an important asset.

Technically, fractions are rational numbers that express the division quotient (a/b) of one number "a" by a non-zero number "b." Initially, fractions are understood as parts of a whole rather than numbers which answer the question "how much?" or "what is the share?" Later, the idea of fraction-as-a-number emerges, particularly when students are exposed to measurement examples and problems.

The concept of "fraction" rates among the most challenging for children and often remains difficult well into adult life. Compounding this challenge has been inappropriate teaching of fractions. Learners are often introduced to the rules and algorithms for handling fractions well ahead of any fundamental understanding of the concept itself and its relationships. It is important to provide some basic understanding before developing any rules or procedures.

Figure 7.1 shows how the relationships included in fractional concepts can be quite difficult to identify. The concept of fraction includes (a) equal-sized parts of a region, a length, or a set; (b) the concept of unit or whole; and (c) the relationship between the parts and the unit.

Each of these represents one-third

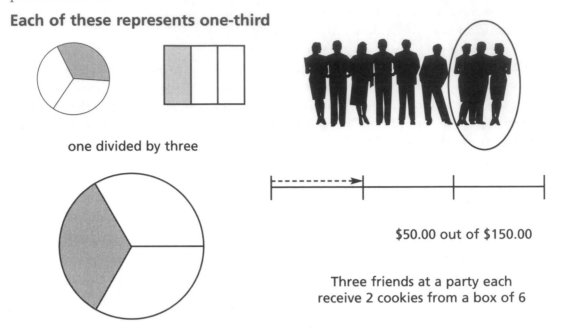

one divided by three

$50.00 out of $150.00

Three friends at a party each
receive 2 cookies from a box of 6

Figure 7.1 *The complicated concepts of "fraction"*

Many children begin their study of fractions in a deficit position, having learned that "half" is just one of two parts. You often overhear a child saying that he or she wants the "larger half" of a pizza or muffin. In fractions, we deal with equal-sized parts regardless of their shape. This characteristic of fractions is, on its own, sometimes difficult to understand. Figure 7.2 demonstrates fractions and non-fractions, based on the distinguishing feature of equal-sized parts. When forming fractions with sets of items such as trees, cookies, or children, the size of the individual items may not be important. However, the number of items in each part must be equal (compare Figure 7.2 (j) and (l)).

The definition of what constitutes the unit or whole, to which the parts are compared, is quite arbitrary. If working with egg cartons, each carton could be considered the unit, or a set of cartons might be the whole with individual cartons representing parts of the whole set. Parts of pizzas or chocolate bars can be further divided into equal parts, but if one loses sight of the original unit or whole, describing a fractional part becomes confusing and misleading.

Finally, fractions describe relationships between the equal parts and the unit or whole. As such, the top number (the numerator) represents the number of equal parts being considered or counted. The bottom number (the denominator) represents the total number of equal parts that make the unit or whole thing. For example, use the fraction 3/4 to describe part of a dollar. This means that four equal parts make the whole dollar and three of those parts are being considered. This relationship is the foundation to understanding fractions and can be used to illuminate many relationships and operations with fractions.

Describing 4/5 as four parts out of the five equal parts that make up a unit expresses a fundamental understanding of fractions.

When establishing the initial understanding of fractions, we suggest that you use the phrases "top number" and "bottom number" rather than the technical terms of "numerator" and "denominator." The technical terms have only obscure connections to their meanings in fractions. Even many adults use mnemonic devices to remember that the denominator is the bottom number; they do not know that "denominator" is related to "denomination," which signifies the name of a type of thing which is the nature of the bottom number. Few know that the root of numerator is found in "enumerate," to count, which suggests that the top number is the number of parts counted or considered.

The terms "top number" and "bottom number" are more descriptive than the technical terms of "numerator" and "denominator."

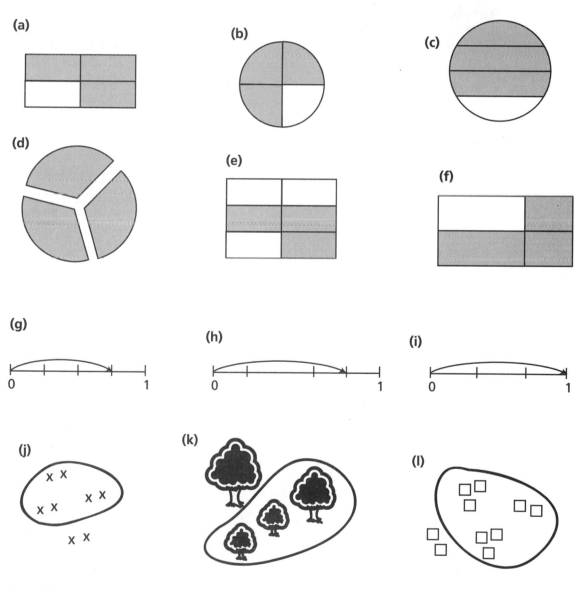

FIGURE 7.2 *Which diagrams show 3/4? (a, b, g, and j, and k if the number of trees matters rather than the size of the trees)*

Fraction symbols can also have several other meanings. They can represent ratios, e.g., the symbol 2/5 meaning the ratio of 2 to 5, such that there are 2 black marbles in every group of 5 marbles or even that there are 2 black marbles and 5 other kinds of marbles in each grouping of 7 marbles. Fractional symbols can also show division, e.g., 7/8 means to divide 7 by 8. These other uses of fractional symbols add a further dimension of difficulty to fractions, confusing those students who are not grounded in the use of fractions to represent the relationship of parts to wholes.

Special considerations in teaching fractions to low achievers

The language of fractions is already part of the experience of low achievers before they encounter any symbolic representations. Children hear or use terms such as "half" and "quarter" long before they can recognize or write the symbols 1/2 or 1/4. Therefore, to build on existing understandings, use the words first and relate them to everyday experiences. Real-life situations, concrete and pictorial representations, words, and symbols all need to be connected conceptually in the mind of the student. Introduce the symbols only when the concepts are secure using the words normally spoken in everyday usage. Figure 2.1 shows how these aspects of the language of fractions are connected as they are for operations and other mathematical concepts and principles.

> To build conceptual understandings, use the words for those fractions found in common experiences. Instead of writing "1/3," write "one third."

Because the word "whole" might be confused with "hole," it is advisable to use the term "unit." Talk about the unit being split or divided into equal parts, of the bottom number being the number of equal parts in one unit, etc. From their work with base-ten blocks where the individual piece is called the unit piece, students may already be familiar with unit as a term meaning indivisible or whole.

Low achievers need to develop the concept of fractional parts: halves, thirds, fourths, fifths and so on. In order to consider any part a fraction, there are two fundamental requirements: (a) the correct number of parts must make up the unit and (b) each of the parts must be the same size (area, length, or quantity) but not necessarily the same shape. You may need to use many examples of fractional and non-fractional parts from common experiences and concrete models and representations to help students understand these two requirements.

You could use a real pizza or a model of one. Cut it in two equal parts. Ask students if they know the name of the fractional part (hold one up). If they do, ask why it is called a half. Ask how many halves there are. If they do not know the name of the fractional part, explain the name and ask them why they think it is called a half. Ask students how many halves there are. Continue to cut the pizza into fourths and then eighths asking the same questions. If students notice that two-fourths is the same as one-half, do not discourage them by ignoring their discovery, but do not become too complicated or abstract.

Help low achievers learn which fractions represent greater and lesser quantities, especially when dealing with sale items, parts of commodities like pizzas and chocolate bars, and sets of things. A sense of size is also crucial for estimation and approximation skills. When comparing the different fractional parts of the same region or set, lead students to notice that the larger the denominator, the smaller the size of the fractional part. This relationship should be learned, not memorized, with student-made explanations and repeated exposure to fractions. This will give them an opportunity to reason mathematically and delve further into the concept of fractions.

The question needs to be answered, "Why is the size of the fractional part smaller if the bottom number is larger?" In this case, the assumption is that the numerator remains constant. For example, 3/5 is larger than 3/8 which is larger than 3/10. The students need to understand and be able to explain that because the denominator indicates the number of pieces that make up the unit: the more pieces, the smaller each will be. It is not enough to know this by rote; students should discover this relationship. Activities that lead to this understanding are presented later in this chapter.

Please note that although we use the terms numerator and denominator when explaining fractions, we still believe it is best, when teaching, to speak of the top number and the bottom number.

Comparing Fractions

It is more difficult to compare fractions in their symbolic form than in graphic representations or as models. Students succeed if they have a solid grounding in the fundamentals and the connections they themselves make between models of fractions, the names, and the symbols. In this section we deal with comparing fractions in their symbolic form. We assume that students have already compared representations and models of fractions successfully.

The most straightforward comparison is between different numbers of equal-sized fractional parts. For example, 2/5 is smaller than 3/5 because the size of the pieces is the same but there are more pieces in 3/5 than in 2/5. Again, it is more important for students to discover this relationship themselves than to have it pointed out. Furthermore, these relationships can be instilled early on, when words and models are used to teach about fractions. The students' thinking and their efforts to see the connections are more valuable than simple rote memorization of the specific relationship.

Ask students to compare the sizes of fractions with the same number of different-sized parts, as in 3/8 and 3/5. They must learn to recognize that 3/8, even with the larger denominator, is the smaller of the two fractions. When the unit is divided equally into eighths, each piece is smaller than when the same unit is divided equally into fifths.

Two other comparisons are also accessible using a conceptual approach, both comparing fractions to benchmarks of 0, 1/2, and 1. Only attempt this with those students who can compare fractions using the above methods. By comparing both 3/7 and 5/8 to 1/2, students can determine that 5/8 is greater than 3/7. By examining the numerator and denominator, they find that 3/7 is less than 1/2 and 5/8 is greater than 1/2. Similarly, students can figure out that 5/4 is greater than 1 and 7/8 is less than 1, making 5/4 the greater of the two.

Finer distinctions can be made using benchmark fractions. Students can tell that 3/4 is less than 9/10 since 3/4 is 1/4 away from 1 and 9/10 is only 1/10 away from 1. Since 9/10 is closer to 1, it is the greater of the two. This kind of reasoning is encouraged in the activities in this chapter.

> Comparing fractions by building on the fundamental definition helps students consolidate their understanding of fractions.

Finally, some fractions (for example, 17/29 or 38/51) do not lend themselves to such conceptual approaches. Many of these are rarely encountered in real life and may not be suitable learning targets for low achievers. However, some fractions may arise while working on a project or in a conversation which are too complex for these conceptual methods. For these rare cases, students can learn to convert a common fraction to a decimal fraction using a calculator, by dividing the denominator into the numerator. Decimal fractions are much easier to compare. This skill can be taught at the same time as the other conceptual comparisons, as a check or verification of their thinking.

Some students may want to use the calculator exclusively when comparing fractions, just like some want to use the calculator for every calculation instead of being judicious in its use. Students need to work through the comparisons conceptually as much to reinforce the understanding as for the result, so discourage them from over-using the calculator. Often, once the skill has been practiced, they find the conceptual approach faster and more convenient than the calculator method. Demonstrate this while dealing with the simpler comparisons.

Adding and Subtracting Fractions

With the proper conceptual understandings and practice with the relationship between the numerator and denominator, all students can be successful at adding and subtracting fractions. The easiest calculations involve fractions with the same denominator. Low achievers can use models and real-life situations to reason why one-fifth plus three-fifths equals four-fifths. If they have learned that the name "fifth" indicates the type or size of the fractional part, then the operation reads a little like "one apple plus three apples equals four apples." Introduce this to students early in their experiences with fractions. If they have begun to use the symbols for fractions, temporarily revert to using the words, with or without concrete models or representations, when adding for the first time. The students may find the operation easier to understand this way.

> Low achievers can learn to add and subtract fractions.

> Changing between improper and mixed fractions helps reinforce newly acquired understandings of top number and bottom number.

Once the concept of adding fractions has been learned using models, representations, and words, student can parallel the words, pictures, or models with the symbols and explain the reasoning by referring to the top number and bottom number. They should be able to explain why the top number changes and the bottom number stays the same.

In some situations, the fraction is greater than one unit (whole). We can express this as an "improper fraction" (8/3) or as a "mixed fraction" or "mixed numeral" (2 2/3). Changing from improper to mixed fractions is a frequent complication when adding and subtracting fractions. However, this manipulation can be better managed using a conceptual approach rather than a rule or procedure. When students add 5/8 and 7/8, they may wonder what the answer 12/8 means. Using their understandings of top and bottom numbers, students can reason that they now have 12 pieces and only 8 pieces make a unit, so they have one complete unit and 4 left-over pieces, making 1 and 4/8. Reverse the procedure for some subtraction problems where, for example, 4/5 is subtracted from 1 and 2/5. The one and two-fifth units can be rewritten as 7/5 (by reasoning that the 1 unit can be expressed as 5/5) and then the 4/5 is subtracted to yield 3/5.

Understanding equivalent fractions helps the student add and subtract fractions with unlike denominators. Using appropriate models, students can discover that the same part of a region, length, or set can have different names and that these are related, in fact "equivalent." The equivalent fraction chart (see Figure 7.3 on page 135) shows these names in a convenient package that can be used to solve fraction problems. Give the students the time and encouragement to discover what equivalent fractions are, rather than simply giving them the chart or the algorithm and telling them what to do. Once they have some experience with the concept of "equivalent fractions," the chart becomes a useful aid to understanding. The chart is given with Target 12.

In real life, students will encounter fractions not found in the equivalent fraction chart. These fractions are probably of limited use in real life and there is little sense in spending huge amounts of time for scant payoff. Nevertheless, students do have some strategies to help them with necessary computations. They can estimate the size of the addition or subtraction by comparing the fractions to the benchmarks of 0, 1/2 and 1. In the case of $17/20 + 5/12$, students could reason that 17/20 is very close to 1 and 5/12 is very close to 1/2. Therefore, the sum would be close to but less than 1 and 1/2, maybe 1 and 1/4 (which happens to be just 1/60 less than the actual answer). These types of estimates are adequate for such obscure fractions, and insisting on the exact answer is often irrelevant.

Don't spend lots of time helping students master computations of unusual common fractions — whether low achievers or not.

One strategy to help low achievers in these rare cases is to convert the common fractions to decimal fractions using a calculator, and then add. The students master the conversion process when learning how to compare fractions, so the leap to using that skill to add difficult fractions is not huge. Finally, they could use a calculator which handles common fractions and treat the problem as one of the addition or subtraction relationships learned for whole numbers.

Converting to Decimal Fractions

The last three learning targets concern the conversion to decimal fractions. Target 15 deserves special mention. Students need reference points for the conversion of common to decimal fractions and the money system provides the best model for that. Through frequent use and practice, students should be able to remember the decimal equivalents for 1/4, 1/2, and 3/4. These later serve as reference points for other conversions, helping the students check the reasonableness of their answers. When they know that 1/2 is 0.5, students can be taught to recognize that 3/8 (less than 1/2) cannot possibly be greater than 0.5.

Concluding Comments

With the right kind of instruction, low achievers are able to master many skills and concepts in the study of fractions. These skills and concepts need to be linked to real situations and concrete models to bring them closer to the experiences of the students. The important outcome is not the complexity or difficulty of the operations or concepts that are

Do not become impatient: stress quality of learning not quantity of calculations mastered.

learned by rote, but the depth of understanding achieved by the students. Do not become impatient with the pace of learning or the seeming lack of progress measured in numbers and kinds of problems solved. Instead, measure success in the conceptual understandings created and reinforced which will allow students to function with confidence and to continue learning as they encounter situations with fractions in their daily lives.

Specific learning targets for common fractions

These targets are arranged from beginning concepts to more complex understandings. The most appropriate progression throughout is from fractional parts of rectangular and circular regions (region models), to lengths, and then to sets of objects as shown in Target 1. We have not repeated this sequence for all the targets but usually the same progression is needed.

> It is important to build solid conceptual understandings before introducing symbols and algorithms.

These teaching targets are cross-referenced to the appropriate activities given later in this chapter. The activities are also cross-referenced to these teaching targets.

Fraction Targets 1–6

The student should be able:

1a. To identify and name fractional parts, given a circular (or rectangular) region model or representation that is divided into equal parts (i.e., 2, 3, 4, 5, 6, 8, 10, or 12).

1b. To identify and name fractional parts, given a strip of paper that is divided into equal parts (i.e., 2, 3, 4, 5, 6, 8, 10, or 12).

1c. To identify and name fractional parts, given a set of markers that is divided into equal groups (i.e., 2, 3, 4, 5, 6, 8, 10, or 12).

2. To divide a rectangular region model or representation into equal parts and name the fractional parts. (Repeat for lengths and sets.)

3. To write in words and symbols the various fractional parts of a strip of paper divided into equal parts. (Repeat for regions and sets.)

4. To identify fractional parts of a common fraction written with symbols and a model divided into the appropriate parts.

5. To explain the meaning of the numerator and denominator of the fractional symbols, given a model divided into fractional parts. (Use the terms "top number" and "bottom number" when working with the students, at least initially.)

6. To distinguish between fractional and non-fractional parts, given the appropriate models, by identifying unequal fractional parts and parts that do not make the unit.

> These targets cover the basic conceptual understandings of fractions. See Activities 7.1, 7.2, and 7.3.

Fraction Target 7

7. To compare fractions conceptually (i.e., using the meaning of the numerator and denominator), given fractional symbols alone: (a) more of the same kind of parts, (b) same or lesser number of smaller sized parts, and (c) more or less than benchmark fractions.

> Target 7 involves comparing fractions. See Activities 7.4 and 7.5.

Fraction Targets 8–13

These targets relate to skills of adding and subtracting fractions. See Activities 7.2 and 7.6.

8. To identify mixed numerals and improper fractions, given the appropriate models as reference.
9. To change the notation of fractions from improper fractions to mixed numerals and back, given appropriate models as reference.
10. To identify and explain the symbols for mixed and improper fractions using references to the meaning of the numerator and denominator and to change from one form to the other.
11. To add and subtract fractional parts with like denominators, given the appropriate models.
12. To identify and list equivalent fractions, given an equivalent fraction chart (see Figure 7.3).
13. To add or subtract fractions with unlike denominators, given an equivalent fraction chart.

1	2	3	4	5	6	7	8	9	10
2	4	6	8	10	12	14	16	18	20
3	6	9	12	15	18	21	24	27	30
4	8	12	16	20	24	28	32	36	40
5	10	15	20	25	30	35	40	45	50
6	12	18	24	30	36	42	48	54	60
7	14	21	28	35	42	49	56	63	70
8	16	24	32	40	48	56	64	72	80
9	18	27	36	45	54	63	72	81	90
10	20	30	40	50	60	70	80	90	100

FIGURE 7.3 *Equivalent fraction chart. Any two numbers in a column could represent a fraction. Equivalent fractions are found in the same rows. For example, select 3/5 in the left column. Move one column to the right in the same rows and you get the equivalent fraction 6/10. Move over three columns and get 12/20. This works for improper fracions as well. Select 35/15 in column 5. Some equivalent fractions are 28/12 and 7/3.*

Fraction Targets 14–16

These targets involve conversions to decimal fractions and adding fractions using a calculator. See Activity 7.7.

14. To write decimal equivalents for 1/4, 1/2, 3/4, and 4/4, given coin models or base-ten blocks.
15. To convert selected simple common fractions to decimal fractions using a calculator.
16. To compare, add, and subtract common fractions by first converting to decimal fractions with the use of a calculator.

Modify these games and tasks to meet the needs of your own students.

Suggested activities

From the following games and activities, select those that provide your low-achieving students with some purposeful learning activities. All these activities are highly recommended but some have not been tried specifically with groups of low achievers. The variations provided are only examples to alert you to other possibilities. Prior instruction on the concepts may be necessary as the activities may not be the best introduction to the skills and learning targets. Suggestions for teaching these fraction concepts are given earlier in this chapter.

These games can be played with partners. This may slow down the game but increases the opportunity for students to talk about mathematics as they decide what to do. As mentioned in Chapter 2, dialogue is extremely valuable in helping students think through their reasoning process.

Building fraction concepts. Targets 1–4.

Activity 7.1 What Am I?

Materials

Large 5 by 5 grid paper with rectangular and circular regions divided into halves, thirds, fourths, fifths, etc. drawn into each space (as in a BINGO card). Instead of markers, clear plastic covers and grease pencils can be used. Paper or cardboard chips with a fraction name written on each one.

Method

Students choose a sheet and prepare for the game. The teacher pulls out one of the fraction names (or lets a student do it) and students mark the squares that show the region divided into the stated parts. A winner can be declared when the designated line or pattern is filled in.

Variations

Use diagrams of lengths, number lines, and sets for the fraction sheets.

Show the fraction symbol as you call out the words, or leave out the words when students are ready to use the symbolic representation alone.

For added difficulty, the teacher can call out the fractional name of the shaded (or indicated) part. For example, instead of just looking for a region divided into fifths, the students would be required to find the diagram that showed two-fifths.

Small groups of students can play the game on their own, with one student pulling the fraction name out of the hat or all taking turns.

Sheets can feature regions or sets that have been divided into fractional parts but not shaded. Students must complete the diagram with the correct number of parts. For example, if the fraction three-fourths were called, students would find a representation of fourths and then shade three of them. There is some strategy to this version as students have some liberty in selecting which of the incomplete "fourths" diagrams to shade.

Activity 7.2 I Spy

The advantage of this game is that all participants practice and consolidate their skills of recognizing and naming fractional parts. Worthwhile discussion can result from considering the appropriateness of certain choices.

This activity helps build fraction concepts. Targets 1–5, 8.

Materials

Various models and representations of fractional parts with some parts shaded (or otherwise distinguished from the other parts of the unit). Use circular or rectangular regions, lengths of string or paper strips, or even sets of objects, depending on the desired difficulty and the readiness of the students.

Method

This game can be played in pairs, small groups, or demonstrated with the whole class.

One student says, for example, "I spy one-third" and the partner or next student responds by finding an example of one-third from the collection of materials. The student finding the spied fraction explains the meaning of the top number and bottom number to the satisfaction of the other students. The others in the game must agree, or can appeal to the teacher who uses the disagreement to reinforce the correct concepts.

Variations

The student calling "I spy" can write the fractional name using symbols and/or say it with words. Mixed and improper fractions can be included in the models.

Activity 7.3 Will the Real Fractions Please Stand Out!

Materials

Numerous examples and representations of fractional parts grouped in fourths, fifths, etc., with non-fractional parts included as distracters. Non-fractional parts should include (a) regions, lengths, and sets divided into unequally sized parts and (b) parts that do not make up the unit. Figure 7.2 contains examples of fractional and non-fractional parts designed to help students distinguish between the two and refine their understanding of fractions. (Use Figure 7.2 as a model when constructing sets of examples and distractors.)

Distinguishing among fractional and non-fractional parts is the ultimate test of understanding what a fraction is. Target 6.

Method

One student reads the directions that accompany one set of examples, such as, "Find the examples of fifths." The other students, in turn, identify from the examples the correct representations of fifths and explain why the incorrect ones are not fifths.

Variations

Begin with parts of regions, both circular and rectangular, and then move on to lengths and sets of objects. At first, confine the incorrect examples to either unequal parts or parts that do not make up a unit, then, when students are ready, combine the misleading attributes for a further challenge.

Activity 7.4 That Was Close!

This activity helps students estimate the size of fractional parts. Target 7.

Materials

Large 3 by 3 grid paper with rectangular and circular regions drawn in each square. The regions are divided into halves, thirds, fourths, fifths, etc. with parts shaded or colored (as in a BINGO card). Instead of markers, clear plastic covers and grease pencils can be used. Make a three-way spinner with the symbols 0, 1/2, and 1 marked on it.

Method

Students choose a sheet and prepare for the game. The teacher (or a designated student) spins for the values 0, 1/2, or 1 and students mark one square that shows a region divided into parts that is close to the selected value. For example, if 0 is spun, a region showing 1/5 could be marked since 1/5 is closer to 0 than it is to 1/2 or 1. A winner is declared when the designated line or pattern is filled in. That student then explains why he or she thought those fractions were close to the "spun" values.

Variations

Use diagrams of lengths, number lines, and sets for the fraction sheets. Use diagrams with the symbols next to them for association, or use just the symbols when working with more advanced students. You can also use the 5 by 5 grid from Activity 7.1. Small groups of students can play the game on their own with one student spinning for the values or they can take turns.

Activity 7.5 What a Card!

In this activity students compare fractional parts using benchmark values of 0, 1/2, and 1. Target 7.

Materials

Sets of cards with fractions written in symbols. One deck could include the following fraction symbols: 1/8, 2/8, 4/8, 7/8, 8/8, 1/4, 2/4, 3/4, 4/4, 1/3, 2/3, 3/3, 1/2, 2/2. Another deck could include: 1/6, 2/6, 3/6, 4/6, 5/6, 6/6, 1/4, 2/4, 3/4, 4/4, 1/3, 2/3, 3/3, 1/2, 2/2. Having multiple copies of some (if not all) of these cards is recommended.

Method

Students shuffle one deck of cards and deal face-down an equal number among two or three players. Together, students turn over their first cards and compare their sizes using the 0, 1/2, and 1 references if necessary. The player with the largest fraction wins, collects the card from each student, and places them at the bottom of his or her own stack of fraction cards. If there is a tie, the students play their next cards and the winner takes all. The game ends when time expires or when one player has won a predetermined number of the cards. If students disagree or are not sure which fraction is the greatest, the problem can be appealed to the teacher who can use this as a teaching moment.

Variations

The cards showing 9/8, 7/6, 5/4, 4/3, 3/2 may be added to the decks when students show an understanding of these simple improper fractions (see Targets 8 and 9).

Activity 7.6 Big Deal!

Materials

The sets of cards from Activity 7.5. Equivalent fraction chart (see Figure 7.3).

All students can add and subtract simple common fractions. Targets 8–13.

Method

Each team consists of two students, and the number of teams depends on the number of cards and the group dynamics. The cards are dealt out to all the students (two stacks per team). The students on each team turn up the first card of each stack and add them. The teams compare sums and the largest sum takes all the cards. Play continues until time expires or one team is eliminated.

Variations

Begin with fraction cards with the same denominator. Move on to fraction cards which can be compared using the equivalent fraction chart.

Activity 7.7 On Your Marks!

This activity is better suited to older, more advanced students who may encounter fractions that cannot easily be compared or added. Over several weeks or months, the students can compile a list of these fractions as they encounter them in daily life. Consequently this activity may not immediately follow the others. It is more important to wait until the students' experiences present the need for learning in this area than to try to teach skills without a meaningful context.

This activity helps students compare, add, and subtract fractions using decimal equivalents or approximations. Targets 15 and 16.

Materials

Calculators; a student-generated list of unusual fractions that were encountered in everyday life.

Method

Write each unusual fraction (those that do not fit the equivalent fraction chart, Figure 7.3) on a slip of paper or card. Randomly select two and display them on the board. Working in pairs, students attempt to add or subtract the fractions by first converting them to decimal fractions. The teacher records the time it takes for the whole class to complete the exercise. When students finish, they may help other pairs. Another two fractions are selected and the process repeated. Students try to beat their previous time, setting a new record.

Variations

Ask some students to explain how they arrived at an answer as a check against a few students doing all the work while the rest are spectators. A consequence can be included such as adding seconds to the group's score if the chosen student or students cannot explain their work. Another variation is to change partners between rounds of the game.

Key teaching points

- Use familiar and meaningful models of fractions such as equal sharing among friends or parts of regions, lengths, and sets.
- Show connections among words, mathematical symbols, concrete and pictorial representations, and real-life situations.
- Allow time for students to think about what fractions mean; help them to verbalize their new understandings.
- Use the words "top number" for numerator and "bottom number" for denominator when working with students.

 QUESTIONS FOR DISCUSSION WITH COLLEAGUES

1. How has the previous learning of fractions affected the ability of students to understand the concepts in a fundamental way? How much relearning of fractions is needed to ensure the solid conceptual understanding outlined by the targets?

2. How can everyday encounters with fractions be made a part of students' experience in mathematics instruction?

3. Are the target statements adequate descriptions of what it means to understand and work with fractions for this age range of low achievers? Are these targets realistic? How do they compare with the local curriculum targets for children of that age? What are the implications of any discrepancies?

4. What improvements or modifications can you make to the activities that might increase the learning opportunities for your students?

8
Money:
A Sample Unit

Introduction

Handling money with confidence and accuracy is clearly a key component of everyday numeracy. In this book we have emphasized the use of money as an effective and meaningful context for students to experience concepts of number and number operations. So, in this final chapter, we outline a sample unit on the topic of money for an imaginary class of students in the 9–11 years age range who find mathematics very challenging. The suggestions here show how some of the principles outlined in this book can be put into practice. Although we have in mind a low-achieving class, the procedures for organization and suggestions for activities could be adapted to a mixed-ability class containing a smaller group of students whose achievement in mathematics is low.

This unit contains sufficient material for several weeks of mathematics in a normal school timetable. There is no ideal way to construct a sample unit in mathematics. However teachers (and student teachers in particular) may find the following headings a useful framework:

PRINCIPLES OF PROCEDURE: The principles of procedure guide the selection of materials and the organization of the student's learning experiences.

TARGETS: Targets are statements of learning outcomes that can readily be assessed. They should cover knowledge, skills, understanding, and (possibly) application.

ACTIVITIES: A collection of learning experiences, activities may be selected at appropriate times for particular groups of students. Some activities are for the whole class, some for small groups, and some for individual or paired work. Some may focus on particular targets, while others may emphasize the type of experience of mathematics being provided for the student.

MATERIALS: It is important to list any materials required for the planned activities and to ensure that they are available.

ORGANIZATION: Consider how the class will be organized to participate in the proposed activities.

LESSON PLANS: It is rarely possible to plan more than the first lesson for any unit in detail, simply because plans for subsequent lessons will depend on what learning took place and what difficulties occurred in earlier lessons.

Principles of procedure

A common topic

First of all, the "unit" is based on the principle of the whole class focusing on a common topic for a number of weeks. This allows some whole-class teaching and activities, although whole-class activities inevitably have shortcomings because of the range of student competencies. However, the exposition and explanation of important ideas and procedures provides significant benefits to the entire class.

Small-group activities

We suggest that most activities be undertaken by small groups of students. Small-group activities, one of the themes in this book, give opportunities for students to use and develop mathematical language. Many of these activities are simple games, providing both a meaningful context and a purpose for the students to engage with mathematics.

Grouping

How you form the student groups will vary from one class to another. If the class has a wide range of mathematical ability, grouping children according to ability may be appropriate. With a low-achieving class, such as the one envisioned in this unit, we propose a flexible grouping system: sometimes grouping children on a friendship basis, sometimes with an eye to their particular mathematical needs. Occasionally, it is helpful for a less able student to work with a more able one. If you have students whose poor social behavior is a major consideration, judge their mood each day to determine who they should work with, or even if it would be more helpful for them to work individually. Also be aware of boys' tendency to take control when a mixed-sex group is working with a computer or other technological equipment. If this occurs, consider single-sex groupings.

Individual or paired work

During the unit, also allow students to engage in individual work to consolidate and practice important skills. However, it is often more effective to have students working in pairs rather than individually, so that they can support each other in interpreting and carrying out their instructions.

Varied demands

In any lesson, students may be engaged in several different activities. Therefore, employ activities that vary in the demands made on you. In each lesson, make one group of children the main focus of your attention. While working to move this group forward in their understanding and mastery of mathematical skills, engage other groups in activities that consolidate and extend previous learning, without the need for much input from you.

Targets and assessment

The unit contains a statement of realistic and relevant targets, covering knowledge, skills, understanding, and to some extent, application. Build into each lesson plan one or more opportunities for assessing the students in a group against some of these targets. You could do this by sitting with them and engaging them in discussion of some mathematical problems. Occasional short written tests of specific knowledge can also be used.

Purposeful activities

The emphasis on targets and assessment is balanced by an equal emphasis on providing the students with purposeful activities in meaningful contexts. The topic of money inevitably provides meaningful contexts, such as shopping, earning, and fund-raising. Within these contexts, some purposeful activities should be developed, including simulations and role play. If possible, incorporate a project in which the students can use math to make something happen, for example, planning an event or solving a real problem.

Language development

Some activities in this chapter focus specifically on the development of important language structures in the context of money, particularly the language of comparison (e.g., "cheaper than," "more expensive than").

Targets

Many of the targets we focus on during this unit were outlined in previous chapters, because money has been identified as an important context for the development of numeracy. Therefore, this unit covers many of the place-value targets outlined in Chapter 4, which propose that using 1¢, 10¢ and $1 coins helps establish the place-value principles. In particular, Targets 26–31 in Chapter 4 relate to money notation. In Chapter 6, the targets gave priority to the context of money when teaching the students to recognize various models of each operation of addition, subtraction, multiplication, and division. As a result in this unit, learning to choose the appropriate operation to enter on a calculator is an important focus. Many of the targets for developing confidence with number, also outlined in Chapter 6, can be experienced in a meaningful way through activities with money, such as buying and selling.

Here, we include additional important targets, specifically related to handling money in practical, realistic situations. The students should be able:

1. To recognize and state the values of the coins and bills in common currency: 1¢, 5¢, 10¢, 25¢, $1, $5, $10, $20, and $2 in Canada.
2. To state and show practically the equivalences between each coin or bill and smaller denominations. (For example, 10¢ = two 5¢ = ten 1¢.)
3. To put out in coins and bills, using the smallest possible number of coins and bills, any given sum of money up to $10.00.
4. To exchange any given collection of coins and bills for the smallest possible number of coins and bills, up to a value of $10.

5. To find, state, and record the value of any given collection of coins and bills, up to a value of $100.
6. To give change from 10¢, 25¢, 50¢, $1, $2, $5, $10, practically, by adding on.
7. To keep an orderly record of income, expenditure, and balance.

Activities

Whole class activities

These activities are designed to involve all the children in the class, thus providing opportunities for discussion, explanation, and clarification of key ideas within the topic.

Activity 8.1 Estimate Cost

Some students are not given much responsibility for handling money at home. They often display little sense of the value of money and what things cost. For example, one student did not know whether a new bicycle cost $1, $10, or $100. This activity can help to remedy this deficiency in their understanding, particularly if you engage them in discussion and comparison of the prices of the various items.

Developing the students' sense of the value of money.

Materials

Various items with their cost; slips of paper for estimates; materials for graphical display of results.

Method

The method is the same as in Activity 5.1 (Estimation class-challenge), used in Chapter 5 for estimating length, weight, capacity, and time, but now adapted to the context of money. For each lesson over a number of days, bring in some item within the students' experience, such as some article of clothing, a radio cassette-player, an item of food or drink, a book, or a digital watch. Have each student write down an estimate of the cost. Process the estimates in the same way as in Activity 5.1, with a different group of students taking responsibility each day for producing the graph showing the class estimates. Have them mark the actual price on the graph as well.

Activity 8.2 Shopping Line

Developing the students' sense of the cost of various purchases, and giving them practice in ordering and in the correct use of money notation.

Materials

Packaging and labels from various purchases with price tags still in place. (If the items have no price tags, mark the prices on small sticky labels.)

Method

Along one wall of the classroom, draw a number line and label it $0.10, $0.20, $0.30, etc. Ask a group of students to sort the packages and labels into ranges of prices, e.g., up to $2, from $2 to $4, etc. Then give each student group one set and ask them to prepare their section of the number line by mounting the packages and labels in the correct locations. Encourage students to bring in packages and labels from home and challenge them to find items to fill in the gaps in the number line.

Activity 8.3 Best-buy Investigation

See Activity 8.16 for a possible precursor to this activity.

Materials

Ask students to gather information about the prices of items (a) bought individually or in multiple packages, (b) sold by weight in various sizes of packages, or (c) sold by volume in various sizes of containers. They could collect packages from their own family shopping with this kind of information. Each student or team also needs a calculator.

> Students use multiplication and division in several contexts to determine the best buy.

Method

Using the price information, students determine the savings achieved by buying multiple packs or larger masses or volumes. This gives a meaningful context for division, multiplication, and subtraction and for learning how to enter sums of money on a calculator and interpret the answers obtained.

For example, one brand of battery can be purchased for 89¢ each, $1.73 for a pack of two, or $3.23 for a pack of four. Students can use this information in two ways. First, using the division key on the calculator, they can determine the price per battery in the multiple packs. This requires careful interpretation of the results produced by the calculator: "1.73 ÷ 2 = 0.865" is a little more than 0.86, or about 86¢ per battery, and "3.23 ÷ 4 = 0.8075" is a little more than 0.80, or about 80¢ per battery. Second, the students could use multiplication to find the cost of purchasing the number of items in the multiple packs if bought separately, and compare this with the price of the multiple packs. This last step gives a context for the comparison model of subtraction. For example, for four batteries at 89¢ each, the calculation entered and the result are "0.89 x 4 = 3.56"; comparing this with $3.23 indicates a saving of $0.33 or 33¢ if bought in a multiple pack.

One group of 11-year-olds were excited to discover that it was actually more expensive to buy a pack of four of a particular kind of chocolate bar than to buy four separately. On their own initiative, they recorded the savings on the multiple pack as –2¢.

When exploring best buys for items sold by weight (such as cereals or chocolate) or those sold by volume (such as lemonade or milk), students may find it easiest to determine how many grams or milliliters are purchased per penny (using their calculators). For example, suppose they can buy a can of lemonade (330 mL) for 29¢, and a bottle (1000 mL) for 55¢, the students might enter on their calculator: "330 ÷ 29 =" and "1000 ÷ 55 =." Their results — that the can has a little more than 11 mL per penny and the bottle contains a little more than 18 mL per penny — tell them that the bottle is better value.

However, if they wish to explore price per unit mass or per unit volume, they will probably not be able to understand the results obtained unless they use the usual supermarket convention of giving "price per 100 g" or "price per 100 mL." For the lemonade example, this would require entering the following key sequences: "29 ÷ 330 x 100 =" and "55 ÷ 1000 x 100 =." With the calculator doing the arithmetic, we find that many students can make sense of this. Because we are working in cents, we use the convention that the digits after the point in the calculator answer represent "little bits of pennies." The students can interpret the results of "8.7878787" and "5.5" as meaning "a little more than 8¢" (for the can) and "a little bit more than 5¢" (for the bottle) per 100 mL. Consequently, the bottle is the best buy.

Activity 8.4 Planning an Event: Refreshment Stand

This purposeful activity (planning an event) in a meaningful context (fund-raising) will probably require about one week to complete.

Developing and using the skills of handling money.

Method
Invite the class to take on the responsibility for planning and organizing the refreshment stand at the school sports day (or other suitable occasion). During a class discussion, have the students identify what needs to be done and allocate the responsibility for components of the planning to various groups of students. Encourage them to determine what should be sold, predict numbers and quantities, purchase and prepare the items, price the items, negotiate with those organizing the sports day, set up and run the stand, determine the float (money for change) required, handle the sales, make change, and calculate the profit. It may be helpful to build into the project a trial run in the classroom, to practice some of the skills of selling and making change.

Activity 8.5 (Activity 6.5) Turning the Tables

This activity, described in Chapter 6, is included in this unit to strengthen the connections between number facts and the context of money. Please refer to Chapter 6 for the detailed description.

Small group activity

This section includes a number of small-group games described in Chapter 4 as well as three new activities.

Activity 8.6 How Many Ways?

Recognizing values of coins and using the equivalences between different denominations. Targets 1 and 2.

Materials
Play coins or real ones.

Method
A group of students is challenged to find all the possible ways of making a given sum of money, using specified coins. For example:

      Find all the ways of making 19¢ using 1¢, 5¢, and 10¢ coins.
      Find all the ways of making 35¢ using 5¢, 10¢, and 25¢ coins.
      Find all the ways of making $1 using 5¢, 10¢, 25¢, and 50¢ coins.

Students should record their results in a table, showing the numbers of each coins used, as shown in Figure 8.1.

Variation
Groups of students could work together to create the table of all possibilities thus reducing the amount of time needed for this activity.

WAYS OF MAKING $1

50¢	25¢	10¢	5¢
2	0	0	0
1	2	0	0
1	1	2	1
1	1	1	3
0	4	0	0
0	3	2	1

etc...

FIGURE 8.1 *Table for Activity 8.6: How Many Ways?*

Activity 8.7 Shopkeeper

This game is for up to five players, plus one who acts as the "bank manager." Although very simple and obvious, it is very effective and gives opportunities for handling coins in a simulated shopping context (Targets 1 and 2), exchanging equivalent coins (Target 4) and making change (Target 6). Both steps in the game involve the giving and receiving of change. Additionally, students use the operations of addition, subtraction, and multiplication in the context of money.

Handling coins in a shopping context (Targets 1 and 2), exchanging equivalent coins (Target 4), and making change (Target 6).

Materials

A supply of play coins; a calculator for each player; Pack A of cards (see Chapter 4) or some other way of generating single-digit numbers; a second set of cards with an item and a price written on each, for example, "pens at 15¢"; included in this pack are a number of cards with the word "BILL" written on them; a third pack with various sums of money written on them, ranging up to $5, this will give the amounts payable when a BILL card is turned up.

Method

Each player is a shopkeeper. The bank manager (who also acts as a universal customer) gives each a float of $5.55 to begin with. In turn, each shopkeeper turns over a card from each of the first two packs to represent a sale, for example, "7 pens at 15¢." The shopkeeper calculates this amount by whatever means makes sense, using the calculator if desired. The bank manager should check the total on a calculator, and then pay out the appropriate amount of money to the player concerned. Even if a calculator is used, the student is still learning to recognize the operation of multiplication in this context, so an important numeracy skill is being developed. Players should always aim to keep the number of coins in their possession to a minimum, exchanging at the bank whenever possible.

Occasionally, a shopkeeper turns up a card saying "BILL." When this happens the bank manager turns over a card from the third pack to reveal a bill (such as $1.75). The player concerned must then pay this to the bank. If the player is unable to pay a bill, he or she is out of the game, being declared bankrupt. There should very few BILLS in the pack, or small enough amounts on the cards in the third pack, so that bankruptcy happens only occasionally. The first shopkeeper to accumulate $20 is the winner.

Variations

(i) To establish place-value ideas, students can play the game using only 1¢, 10¢, and $1 coins. In this case, require that the students exchange ten 1¢ coins for one 10¢, and ten 10¢ coins for one $1, otherwise the player misses a turn.

(ii) An important version of this game, focusing on Target 7, is played without coins or a bank manager. Instead, using a calculator, students keep a simple record of sales and bills, using three columns for income, expenditure, and balance, like this:

BALANCE	INCOME	EXPENDITURE
5.55	1.05	nil
6.60	1.12	nil
7.72	nil	1.75
5.97	etc	

In the above example, the shopkeeper started with a float of $5.55, sold 7 pens at 15¢ ($1.05) (by drawing cards as above) and 8 chocolate bars at 14¢ ($1.12), then paid out a bill of $1.75. During the process, the student has to recognize the need for entering multiplication, addition, and subtraction on the calculator, and has transformed money notation from cents to dollars. Use this version of the game once the students have had plenty of experience with the version using coins.

Activity 8.8 I Have, Who Has: Change from a Dollar

Materials
A set of cards similar to those prepared for Activity 6.9, with the "questions" being various sums of money (e.g. 46¢, 35¢, 9¢, . . .) and the "answers" being the corresponding change from a dollar (i.e. 54¢, 65¢, 91¢, . . .).

This game, described in Activity 6.9, is adapted to give practice in making change from a dollar.

Method
See Activity 6.9.

Variations
Use dollar notation (i.e., $0.46, $0.35. $0.09, etc.).

The questions could consist of two prices which must be added together (e.g., 35¢ and 17¢, with 48¢ on the back of the card).

Activity 8.9 Role Play

This activity shows how role play can be used to give more purpose to doing mathematics. Give a small group of students the opening section of a script for a short play and invite them to work out the rest of it themselves. They need not produce a written script. Much of the drama can be improvised, provided they agree on the framework of the plot. In order to make this a useful mathematical experience, however, any financial transactions involved must be acted out properly with coins, not just pretended. When they have figured out their scene, the students can present it to the rest of the class.

(**SETTING:** Tracey is sitting at home, counting her savings: she has $3.76. Mom, Dad, and Simon are reading.)

TRACEY: One dollar, two dollars, three dollars, three dollars and fifty, sixty, seventy, seventy-two, seventy-four, seventy-six . . . that's three dollars and seventy-six cents. And we need ten dollars to go on the trip to Medicine Hat next month. I'll never save up enough.

MOM: Ooh, that reminds me. Aunt Mabel is coming by later on. Perhaps you could drop her a hint.

DAD: And here's your allowance, Tracey. (Hands her 50¢)

TRACEY: Thanks, Dad. That's another fifty cents toward the trip.

SIMON: How much do you have saved up now, Trace?

TRACEY: Er, that's three dollars and seventy-six, plus fifty. Four dollars and something.

DAD: Four dollars and thirty-six cents!

MOM: No, George, it's four dollars and twenty-six cents.

DAD: It's thirty-six, I tell you.

MOM: It's twenty-six, George.

DAD: (Getting angry) Thirty-six!

MOM: All right, George, if you say so. (Quietly, to Tracey) It's twenty-six.

DAD: Give the money here, Tracey. (He takes the money and counts it.) Now, look. Three dollars, four quarters make a dollar, that's four dollars and ten, twenty, twenty-six . . . er, four dollars and twenty-six . . . . (slips another ten cents from his pocket into the pile) There you are, four dollars and thirty-six cents!

TRACEY: Thanks, Dad. I knew you were right all along. (Aside) That's another ten cents toward the trip!

SIMON: So, how much more do you need now, Tracey?

TRACEY: Well, I've got four dollars and thirty-six cents, and I need ten dollars altogether ...

DAD: Perhaps this time you'd better use that calculator that Aunt Mabel gave you for your birthday.

TRACEY: (Picking up the calculator): Right, now let's see, how can we work this out? (There is a knock on the door . . .)

Variation

Instead of the opening section of a script, provide the students with a brief description of a situation, for which they must improvise a response and act it out. For example:
A customer in a grocery store does not have enough money to pay for all the goods in the shopping cart.

A group of children find a lost treasure and get a reward which they must share among themselves.

Some newspaper delivery girls and boys go to their manager to ask for a raise.

A shop decides to sell off all its toys at half price.

Again, it is important that in each of these role-play situations, the students handle actual coins (albeit play coins), not just imaginary ones.

Activity 8.10 (Activity 4.2) Race to a Dollar

Activity 8.11 (Activity 4.3) Race to Ten Dollars

Activity 8.12 (Activity 4.13) Spend Ten Dollars

These three games from Chapter 4 focus on the processes of addition and subtraction in the context of money, using 1¢, 10¢, and $1 coins to develop place-value concepts.

Activity 8.13 (Activity 4.12) Win Some, Lose Some

Another small-group game from Chapter 4, this develops the principle of exchange using coins.

Activity 8.14 Money-boxes

This activity is the place-value game Boxes (Activity 4.7), adapted for use with money notation as suggested at the end of Chapter 4.

Individual or paired activities

This section also includes a number of suggestions from previous chapters.

Activity 8.15 Catalogue Shopping

The purpose of this activity is to develop the student's ability to recognize the operations of addition and subtraction in the context of money and to practice the use of money notation when recording purchases. The activity falls into the category of a simulation of a real problem.

> The teacher can personalize each student's task while they practice the operations of addition and subtraction in the context of money.

Materials

A collection of mail-order catalogues brought from home; imitation order forms as shown in Figure 8.2; a calculator for each student.

Method

Set a challenge for each student at a difficulty level appropriate to the child. Do this by filling in numbers in the two boxes at the top of the order form. For example, you might require one student to buy 5 items, spending up to $50, whereas another might be challenged to buy 12 items, spending up to $200. The challenge is for the students to spend as much of their money as possible. Students use their calculators to add up what they have spent so far. Then, by choosing the operation of subtraction, they calculate how much they have left to spend at each stage. When they have decided on their purchases, they complete their order form.

This is a very successful activity with low-achieving students, giving purposeful experience of addition and subtraction in a meaningful context. They usually get very involved in the simulation, showing great determination to spend as much as they possibly can while only choosing things they really want!

ORDER FORM

Choose [   ] items from the catalogue. You may spend up to $ [   ]

Item	Page	Reference number	Price
		Total spent	
		How much left	

FIGURE 8.2 *Imitation order form for catalogue shopping (Activity 8.15)*

Activity 8.16 Best-buy Program

Materials

A personal computer and a program like that shown in Figure 8.3, and a calculator.

> Practicing division in the contexts of money and mass in order to determine the best buy. Useful preparation for Activity 8.3.

Method

Experience suggests that two students is the optimum number working together on a computer. As noted above under Principles of procedure, it may be preferable to have children of the same sex working together on a computer.

The program allows students to practice best-buy shopping in the classroom. In ten questions, they get a choice of two purchases, presented on the screen like this:

CHOOSE EITHER:
1. 340 g for 58¢
       OR
2. 250 g for 26¢

TYPE 1 OR 2

The computer then responds to the student's choice with either "BEST BUY!" or "WORST BUY!" A running total of the number of best buys is kept. A student with a score of 8 or more is judged to be an excellent shopper. Allow low-achieving students to use a calculator, paper, and pencil to help make the decisions. This is done most simply by finding the number of grams purchased per penny, hence gaining experience of choosing the operation of division for an equal-sharing situation in the context of weight divided by money (see Chapter 5).

Variations

You may be able to produce more sophisticated versions of the program given here. Even inexperienced programmers can modify it for their own purposes, for example, change the grams in lines 80 and 90 to milliliters for liquid volume rather than mass. Change the criterion for excellence in line 220 from "S>7" to "S>8" and so on, and write your own messages. Change the "¢" to "$" in lines 80 and 90. To produce different ranges of weights and prices, try putting different numbers in the brackets in the "RND( )" statements in lines 40 and 50 and see what happens.

```
10   S = 0
20   FOR N = 1 TO 10
30   CLS
40   A = RND(100)*10: B = RND(100)*10
50   C = RND(5)*10+RND(5): D = RND(5)*10+RND(5)
60   PRINT:PRINT:PRINT
70   PRINT N;*.CHOOSE EITHER:*:PRINT
80   PRINT *1. ";A;" g for ";C;"p:PRINT "OR"
90   PRINT *2. ";B;" g for ";D;"p"
100  INPUT *TYPE 1 OR 2        *X
110  IF X<>1 AND X<>2 THEN 100
120  IF C/A<D/B AND X=1 THEN 150
130  IF C/A>D/B AND X=2 THEN 150
140  PRINT:PRINT "WORST BUY!":GOTO 170
150  PRINT:PRINT "BEST BUY!"
160  S= S+1
170  PRINT:PRINT: S," best buy(s) so far"
180  PRINT:PRINT:PRINT"PRESS ANY KEY TO CONTINUE"
190  W=INKEY(32767): NEXT N
200  CLS: PRINT: PRINT
210  PRINT S" BEST BUY(S) OUT OF 10":PRINT
220  IF S>7 THEN PRINT "YOU ARE AN EXCELLENT SHOPPER!":STOP
230  IF S<5 THEN PRINT "I WOULDN'T TRUST YOU WITH MY MONEY!":STOP
240  PRINT"NOT TOO BAD, BUT YOU NEED MORE PRACTICE"
250  END
```

FIGURE 8.3 *Best-buy program in BBC-BASIC*

Activity 8.17 School Cafeteria/Tuck-shop

Method

If your school has either a tuck-shop or a cafeteria, arrange for two students each day to help in receiving customers' payments, making change, and counting the revenue at the end of the session. If students know that they are preparing for this responsibility, their commitment to their work in mathematics lessons will increase. Some specific training for the job, using role play, simulated items for purchase, and play coins, could be given beforehand.

Giving students real experience in making change and counting money in a genuine selling situation. Targets 5 and 6.

Activity 8.18 (Activity 6.19) Have Calculator, Will Solve

As described in Chapter 6, this activity develops confidence with important mathematical structures in the context of money, as well as with the associated language patterns. Focus particularly on the following language: increased, reduced, costs more than, costs less than, more expensive, less expensive, cheaper, per, each.

Activity 8.19 "Fuzzy-region" Exercises: Choosing the Operation

Under the heading Fuzzy Regions in Chapter 6 (page 90), we described worksheets each with a series of graded exercises. These allow students to discover for themselves (by exploring keys on their calculators) the mathematical structures of various models of the operations of addition, subtraction, multiplication, and division. You could focus the worksheets on the models of operations that your students find difficult, such as the inverse-of-addition model of subtraction or the inverse-of-multiplication model of division.

Activity 8.20 Money Grids

Adapt Activity 4.10, Grids (see Figure 4.6), for use with money notation to allow practice in simple addition and subtraction. For example, a grid could start with 3.09 in the top left corner and use the two instructions "EARN 2¢" and "SPEND 10¢." A supply of these grids is useful for keeping those students who finish other activities early productively occupied.

Activity 8.21 (Activity 4.15) Money Notation Worksheets

These worksheets, described in Chapter 4, focus on the correct use of money notation, translations between cents and dollars (e.g., 86¢ = $0.86), and the interpretation of calculator results in money calculations.

Activity 8.22 Say, Press, Check, Write: Money

As suggested in Chapter 4, Activity 4.7 can be adapted for use with money notation.

Materials for the unit

To employ the activities listed above, the following materials will be required:
Various items for students to estimate cost (Activity 8.1)

* 12 large sheets of 2-cm squared paper (for graphs, Activity 8.1)
* meter stick
* 2 cm wide strips of colored paper
* pair of scissors
* glue stick
* supply of packages and labels with prices shown (Activity 8.2)
* large supply of play coins, all denominations
* 24 calculators (at least one for every two students)
* 3 sets of packs A and B cards (generating single-digit numbers)
* other packs of cards for Activity 8.7
* account sheets for recording balance, income, and expenditure for a variation in Activity 8.7
* cards for I Have, Who Has game (Activity 8.8, including variations)
* copy of script for role play in Activity 8.9

* copies of statements of situations for Activity 8.9 variation
* pack E: cards for Win Some, Lose Some (Activity 8.13/4.12)
* supply of strips of cardstock with boxes drawn (Activity 8.14/4.7)
* mail-order catalogues (Activity 8.15)
* imitation order forms for mail orders (Activity 8.15, Figure 8.2)
* personal computer with program (Figure 8.3, Activity 8.16)
* cards with layout for Have Calculator, Will Solve (Activity 8.18)
* worksheets with graded exercises for each model of +, −, ×, ÷, in the context of money (Activity 8.19)
* supply of blank grids (Activity 8.20)
* money-notation worksheets (Activity 8.21/4.15)
* worksheets with headings for Say, Press, Check, Write: Money (Activity 8.22)

Organizing the unit

Learning centers

Figure 8.4 shows a simple structure for a typical seventy-minute mathematics lesson for low-achieving 9- to 11-year-olds. The model employed here is that of learning centers, sandwiched between some brief whole-class activities.

10 min	whole-class activity
5 min	organization
20 min	learning centers: small-group and individual or paired work
5 min	interruption
20 min	learning centers continued
10 min	clearing up and whole-class activity

FIGURE 8.4 *A possible structure for a mathematics lesson*

We do not suggest that every lesson should follow this format, simply that this might be a useful model to follow much of the time. The time allocations in Figure 8.4 are, of course, very flexible.

The structure includes about ten minutes at the start of the lesson for a whole-class activity, for example, Activity 8.1 (Estimate Cost) which could be used to focus the class' attention on the topic at hand. Alternatively, you could use this time for a class discussion or question-and-answer session about some key ideas such as the correct way of writing a sum of money using dollar notation or the relationship between cents and dollars.

The bulk of the lesson involves small-group activities and individual (or paired) work. This is referred to as "learning centers." Setting up these centers obviously requires some time (see below).

In the middle of the lesson, we built in an "interruption." In our experience, many students find that 45 minutes working on the same kind of activity is too long. In Chapter 2 we suggested some concessions to accommodate students' difficulties in concentrating on one task for a prolonged time. Therefore, we stop them after 20 minutes or so and do something else for a few minutes. For example, you could deliberately look for a problem or something of interest in some of the students' work, and share and discuss it with the whole class. Sometimes this interruption could be used for a short class game, to show some completed work, for a mental arithmetic test, or even just for a chat about what the children did on the weekend.

The final ten minutes is allocated to cleaning up and a further short period of whole-class activity. This could be used regularly to focus on basic number knowledge, for example, using an activity like Turning the Tables (Activity 8.5).

A framework for the learning centers

Assume that your class consists of 24 students, who we will refer to as A, B, C, . . . X. Assume this class is arranged roughly in order of mathematical ability, with the least able students at the beginning of the alphabet and the more able ones at the end. In Principles of procedure (above), we discussed some ideas for grouping these students for the selection of various activities. These principles can be put into practice using the framework shown in Figure 8.5. This diagram applies to the learning centers, those sections of the lesson given over to the small-group and individual or paired activities, and provides a basic structure for a sequence of four lessons.

Groups

	A–F	G–L	M–R	S–X
Lesson 1	Moving forward	Small-group extension activities	Small-group extension activities	Individual or paired work: consolidating
Lesson 2	Individual or paired work: consolidating	Moving forward	Small-group extension activities	Small-group extension activities
Lesson 3	Small-group extension activities	Individual or paired work: consolidating	Moving forward	Small-group extension activities
Lesson 4	Small-group extension activities	Small-group extension activities	Individual or paired work: consolidating	Moving forward

FIGURE 8.5 *Framework for learning centers for four lessons*

The framework in Figure 8.5 assumes that you have organized the students into four groups, A–F, G–L, M–R and S–X, roughly according to ability. This is a starting point for organization and does not mean that the students work only in these groupings.

Secondly, the framework assumes that the groups will engage in three kinds of activities:

1. Assessment and moving forward: The teacher sits with the group in order to assess and teach them, checking each student's progress against some of the targets, diagnosing difficulties, maybe introducing new material, clarifying ideas previously found difficult, and explaining procedures.
2. Individual or paired consolidation work: The students work individually or in pairs on worksheets, puzzles, or computer activities designed to consolidate their learning based on the teacher's work with them.
3. Small-group extension activities: Students engage in appropriate small-group activities, calling on and extending their mathematical knowledge and skills within the given topic.

As much as possible, activities are selected so that only the group scheduled for assessment and moving forward should make heavy demands on the teacher. In the framework of Figure 8.5, two groups are engaged in small-group extension activities at any one time, so you can be flexible when grouping the students for these activities.

Overall plan

It should be stressed that Figure 8.5 is no more than a basic framework for planning a series of lessons. For example, you could set aside a few lessons for the whole class to engage in Activity 8.3 (Best-buy Investigation) or Activity 8.2 (Shopping Line). Then, toward the end of the topic, perhaps a whole week could be given to the project described in Activity 8.4 (Planning an Event: Refreshment Stand). During this project you will find further opportunity to vary the student groupings, so that some less able students might benefit from working alongside more able friends.

Over twenty days, the unit might develop like this:

Days 1–4:   Learning centers
Day 5:   Whole-class Activity 8.2, Shopping Line
Days 6–9:   Learning centers
Day 10–11:   Whole-class Activity 8.3, Best-buy Investigation
Days 12–15: Learning centers
Days 16–20: Class project (Activity 8.4) Planning an Event: Refreshment Stand

First lesson plan

The proposed plan for the first lesson in the unit is shown in Figure 8.6. This uses the lesson structure outlined above in Figure 8.4.

Opening whole-class activity: Estimate Cost (Activity 8.1)					
Organize learning centers					
ABCDEF Grids. Assessment and moving forward: addition and subtraction models in shopping context.	**GHIR** Activity 8.7: Shopkeeper	**JKLM** Activity 8.13: Win Some, Lose Some	**NOPQ** Activity 8.14: Money-boxes	**STUV** Individual Work, Activity 8.15: Catalogue Shopping	**WX** Organize and graph data from Activity 8.1: Estimate Cost
Interruption: talk about range of estimates from Activity 8.1 at the beginning of the lesson					
Work on dollar notation, Activity 8.20: Money Grids	↓	(possibly swap games)		↓	↓
Clearing up. Show graph for Estimate Cost. Introduce Activity 8.2: Shopping Line. If time, play Activity 8.5: Turning the Tables, with 7 + 8 = 15.					

FIGURE 8.6 *Possible lesson plan*

Opening activity

Introduce the class to Activity 8.1 (Estimate Cost), explaining that they will do this at the start of each lesson for a few days, to see how good they are at estimating the cost of various purchases. After showing the item, ask each student to write down an estimate for the price on a slip of paper. Explain the dollar notation for money and encourage students to write their estimates in this way.

Learning Centers

The learning centers section of this lesson is based on the plan for Day 1 in Figure 8.5: students A–F are the main focus of the teacher's attention for assessment and moving forward; students G–R will participate in small-group activities; and students S–X will engage in individual or paired work.

Students W and X are given responsibility for organizing and graphing the class' estimates for the cost of the article. Since this activity is a regular feature of any work on measurement, these students have done this before with estimates of length, time, capacity, or weight, so will need little instruction. If necessary, provide an example of the kind of graph to be produced. The four other students in this group (S, T, U, and V) can work individually on Catalogue Shopping (Activity 8.15). Because this is a new activity for them, keep it fairly simple to begin with: for example, choose 5 items and spend up to $20.

Students N, O, P, and Q will play the game Money-boxes (Activity 8.14). They are familiar with this game in the original version (Activity 4.7), so will require only a little instruction about playing the same game with dollar notation. Students J, K, L, and M will play Win Some, Lose Some (Activity 8.13/4.12). They also are familiar with their game and will require no more than a reminder of the rules. These two groups could switch activities for the second half of the lesson. Introduce students G, H, I, and R to a new game, Shopkeeper (Activity 8.7). Student R is a fairly competent student and can act as bank manager for this game.

Give students A–F some simple Grids (see Activity 4.10) to keep them purposefully occupied while you get the other groups organized and introduce the new game to students G, H, I, and R. Then, sit with the A–F group and assess their understanding of various models of addition and subtraction in the context of shopping. Place several purchases on the table with prices prominently displayed (in cents only at this stage). Give each student a calculator. Then, go round the group asking questions such as:

How much does it cost to buy these two? What do you enter on your calculator to work this out?

How much more does this cost than that? What do you enter on your calculator to work this out?

How much less does this cost than that? What do you enter on your calculator to work this out?

What is the difference in price between this and that? What do you enter on your calculator to work this out?

If you had 45¢ and wanted to buy this, how much more would you need? What do you enter on your calculator to work this out?

If the shopkeeper reduced this by 25¢, what would it cost? What do you enter on your calculator to work this out?

Note the students' responses to these questions and use them to determine which Calculator Sentences or Graded Exercises worksheets (Activities 8.18 and 8.19) to give them in the next lesson to follow up this assessment.

Also, spend some time with this group on dollar notation, then leave them with some Money Grids (Activity 8.20) while you check on the progress of other groups of children. Keep a supply of Money Grids available as fillers for any students who complete their activity before the end of the allotted time.

Interruption

Half-way through the time allotted to the learning centers, call the students back together for a few minutes. During this time, talk about the range of estimates that students W and X discovered as they organized the data from the opening activity. The actual cost could be disclosed at this point, and estimates that are excessively low or high could be compared with this.

Closing activities

Assuming the graph of the class' estimates is complete, display and discuss it. Challenge the class to try to estimate much closer to the actual cost in future. Introduce the idea for the Shopping Line (Activity 8.2) and ask the class to bring from home labels and packages that show the prices.

If time remains, write "7 + 8 = 15" on the board and play Turning the Tables (Activity 8.5/6.5), asking questions such as:

What is 8 plus 7?

What is 15 take away 8?

What is the difference between 7 and 15?

How much would you pay for a pen costing 7¢ and a pencil costing 8¢?

You have 15¢ and spend 8¢. How much do you have left?

You have 7¢ and want to buy a ruler for 15¢. How much more do you need?

I have 15¢ and you have 8¢. How much less do you have than I have?

 # QUESTIONS FOR DISCUSSION WITH COLLEAGUES

1. If students are consolidating skills through worksheets or puzzles, what are the advantages and disadvantages of their working individually as opposed to working in pairs?
2. What is your view of our suggestion for a planned interruption in the middle of a mathematics lesson?
3. How would you plan the second lesson in this unit?
4. What criteria would you use to evaluate the unit outlined in this chapter?
5. Revisit the questions at the end of Chapter 1 about low-achieving students. What would you say now in the light of what you have read in this book?

Further Reading

Ainscow, M. and Tweddle, D.A. (1979) *Preventing Classroom Failure: An Objectives Approach*. Toronto, ON: John Wiley & Sons.

American Psychological Association (1993) *Learner Centered Psychological Principles: Guidelines for School Redesign and Reform*. Washington, DC: American Psychological Association and the Mid-continent Regional Educational Laboratory.

Ames, R. and Ames, C. (eds.) (1984) *Research on Motivation in Education: Volume 1: Student Motivation*. Orlando, FL: Academic Press.

Barron, L. (1979) *Mathematics Experiences for the Early Childhood Years*. Columbus, OH: Charles E. Merrill Publishing Company.

Bell, A., Burkhardt, H., McIntosh, A. and Moore, G. (1978) *A Calculator Experiment in a Primary School*. Shell Centre for Mathematical Education, University of Nottingham.

Beugin, M.E. (1990) *Coping: Attention Deficit Disorder*. Calgary, AB: Detselig Enterprises.

Biggs, E. (1985) *Teaching Mathematics 7–13: Slow-Learning and Able Pupils*. NFER-Nelson.

Biggs, J.B. (1967) *Mathematics and the Conditions of Learning*. National Foundation for Educational Research.

Blake, G. (1985) "Using maths to make things happen: The mystery of the forgotten shower unit," In T. Booth et al. (eds.) *Preventing Difficulties in Learning*. Basil Blackwell in association with the Open University.

Bley, N.S. and Thornton, C.A. (1981) *Teaching Mathematics to the Learning Disabled*. Rockville, MD: Aspen Publishers, Inc.

Bloom, B.S. (ed.) (1956) *Taxonomy of Educational Objectives: The Classification of Educational Goals: Handbook 1: Cognitive Domain*. David McKay Co.

Bowers, J. (1981) "Excursion to Boulogne," *Struggle: Mathematics for Low Attainers*, no. 4. (ILEA).

Brown, M. (1981) "Number Operations," In K.M. Hart (ed.) *Children's Understanding of Mathematics, 11–16*. John Murray.

Bruner, J., Goodnow, J.J., and Austin, G.A. (1967) *A Study of Thinking*. New York, NY: Science Editions, Inc.

Burns, M. (1984) "The math solution: Using groups of four," In N. Davidson (ed.) *Cooperative Learning in Mathematics: A Handbook for Teachers*, pp. 21–46. Menlo Park, CA: Addison-Wesley.

Cardelle-Elawar, M. (1992) "Effects of teaching metacognitive skills to students with low mathematical ability," *Teaching and Teacher Education*, Vol. 8(2), pp. 109–121.

Carraher, T.C., Carraher, D. and Schliemann, A.D. (1985) "Mathematics in the streets and in schools," *British Journal of Developmental Psychology*, Vol. 3(1).

Carraher, T.C., Schliemann, A.D. and Carraher, D.W. (1988) "Mathematical concepts in everyday life," In G.B. Saxe and M. Gearhard (eds.) *Children's Mathematics. New Directions in Child Development Series no. 41*. San Francisco, CA: Jossey-Bass.

Cathcart, W., Pothier, Y., and Vance, J. (1997) *Learning Mathematics in Elementary and Middle Schools*, 2nd ed. Scarborough, ON: Allyn & Bacon, Canada.

Child, D. (1993) *Psychology and the Child*, 5th ed. London, UK: Cassel.

Clement, M.A. (1980) "Analyzing children's errors on written mathematical tasks," *Educational Studies in Mathematics*, Vol. 11(1).

Cobb, P. (1994) "Constructivism in Mathematics and Science Education," *Educational Researcher*, Vol. 23(7).

Cockcroft, W.H. (chairman) (1982) *Mathematics Counts*. (Report of the Committee of Inquiry into the Teaching of Mathematics in Schools), Her Majesty's Stationery Office.

Cognition and Technology Group at Vanderbilt University (1992) "Anchored instruction in science and mathematics: Theoretical basis, developmental projects, and initial research findings," In R.A. Duschl and R. J. Hamilton (eds.) *Philosophy of Science, Cognitive Psychology, and Educational Theory and Practice*, pp. 244–273. Albany: State University of New York.

Czerneda. J.E. (ed.) (1996) *All Aboard: Cross Curricular Design and Technology Strategies and Activities*. Toronto, Canada: Trifolium Books, Inc.

Davison, D. and Pearce, D. (1988) "Using writing activities to reinforce mathematics instruction," *Arithmetic Teacher* Vol. 35(8), April.

Day, J., French, L., and Hall, L. (1985) "Social influences on cognitive development," In D. L. Forrest-Pressley, G. E. MacKinnon, and T. G. Waller (eds.) *Metacognition, Cognition, and Human Performance*. Orlando, FL: Academic Press

Dees, R.L. (1984) "Cooperating in the mathematics classroom: A user's manual," In N. Davidson (ed.) *Cooperative Learning in Mathematics: A Handbook for Teachers*, pp. 160–200. Menlo Park, CA: Addison-Wesley.

Denvir, B., Stolz, C. and Brown, M. (1982) *Low Attainers in Mathematics 5–16, Policies and Practices in Schools*. (Schools Council Working Paper 72), Methuen.

Department of Education and Science and the Welsh Office (1989) *Mathematics in the National Curriculum*. Her Majesty's Stationery Office.

Dickson, L., Brown, M. and Gibson, O. (1984) *Children Learning Mathematics: A Teacher's Guide to Recent Research*. Holt, Rinehart & Winston.

Dienes, Z. (1960) *Building Up Mathematics*. Hutchinson.

Donaldson, M. (1978) *Children's Minds*. Fontana.

Duncan, A. (1978) *Teaching Mathematics to Slow Learners*. Ward Lock Educational.

Easen, P. (1985) "All at sixes and sevens: The difficulties of learning mathematics," In T. Booth et al. (eds.) *Preventing Difficulties in Learning*. Basil Blackwell in association with the Open University.

French, M. and Landretti, A. (1995) *Attention Deficit and Reading Instruction*. Bloomington, IN: Phi Delta Kappa Educational Foundation.

Gallimore, R. and Tharp, R. (1990) "Teaching mind in society: Teaching, schooling, and literate discourse," In L. Moll (ed.) *Vygotsky and Education*. Cambridge University Press.

Girling, M. (1977) "Towards a definition of basic numeracy," *Mathematics Teaching*, #81.

Glennon, V.J. (1981) *The Mathematical Education of Exceptional Children and Youth: An Interdisciplinary Approach*. National Council for Teachers of Mathematics.

Graham, S. (1994) "Classroom motivation from an attributional perspective," In H.F. O'Neil Jr. and M. Drillings (eds.) *Motivation: Theory and Research*, pp. 31–48. Hillsdale, NJ: Lawrence Erlbaum.

Hart, K.M. (ed.) (1981) *Children's Understanding of Mathematics*, 11–16. John Murray.

Hatfield, M., Edwards, N.T., and Bitter, G. (1993) *Mathematics Methods for the Elementary and Middle School*. Boston, MA: Allyn and Bacon.

Haylock, D.W. (1986) "Mathematical low attainers checklist," *British Journal of Educational Psychology*, #56.

Haylock, D.W. (1987) "Towards numeracy," *Support for Learning*, Vol. 2(2).

Haylock, D.W. (1991) *Teaching Mathematics to Low Attainers, 8–12*. London, UK: Paul Chapman Publishing Ltd.

Haylock, D.W. (1995) *Mathematics Explained for Primary Teachers*. London, UK: Paul Chapman Publishing Ltd.

Haylock, D.W., Blake, G.F. and Platt, J. (1985) "Using maths to make things happen," *Mathematics in School*, Vol. 14(2).

Haylock, D. and Cockburn, A. (1997) *Understanding Early Years Mathematics*. London, UK: Paul Chapman Publishing.

Haylock, D.W. and McDougall, D (1999) *Mathematics Every Elementary Teacher Should Know*. Toronto, ON: Trifolium Books, Inc.

Haylock, D. and Morgans, H. (1986) "Maths to make things happen," *British Journal of Special Education*, Vol. 13(1).

Heide, A. and Henderson, D. (1994) *The Technological Classroom: A Blueprint for Success*. Toronto, Canada: Trifolium Books, Inc. and Irwin Publishing. Second edition in press.

Heide, A. and Stilborne, L. (1999) *The Teacher's Complete & Easy Guide to the Internet, Second Edition*. Toronto, Canada: Trifolium Books, Inc.

Her Majesty's Inspectors of Schools (1984) *Education Observed 2*. Her Majesty's Stationery Office.

Her Majesty's Inspectors of Schools (1978) *Aspects of Secondary Education in England*. Her Majesty's Stationery Office.

Hope, J. (1990) *Charting the Course: A Guide for Revising the Mathematics Program in the Province of Saskatchewan*. Regina, SK: University of Regina and Saskatchewan Instructional Development and Research Unit.

Hope, J. (1993) "How Big is a Whale? and Other Interesting Math Problems," Conference presentation, Sciematics, Saskatoon, SK.

Hughes, M. (1986) *Children and Number: Difficulties in Learning Mathematics*. Basil Blackwell.

ILEA Learning Resources Branch (1985) *Count Me In*. Inner London Education Authority.

Jackson, M., and Canada, R. (1995) "Self-concept and math among potential school dropouts," *Journal of Instructional Psychology*, Vol. 22(3).

Jennings, C. and Di, X. (1996) "Collaborative learning and thinking: The Vygotskian approach," In L. Dixon-Krauss (ed.) *Vygotsky in the Classroom: Mediated Literacy, Instruction and Assessment*. White Plains, NY: Longman Publishers.

Johnson, D.W. and Johnson, R.T. (1984) "Using cooperative learning in math," In N. Davidson (ed.) *Cooperative Learning in Mathematics: A Handbook for Teachers*. pp. 103–125. Menlo Park, CA: Addison-Wesley.

Jones, K. and Charlton, C. (eds.) (1992) *Learning Difficulties in Primary Classrooms: Delivering the Whole Curriculum*. Macmillan Education.

Jones, K. and Haylock, D. (1985) "Developing children's understanding in mathematics," *Remedial Education*, Vol. 20(1).

Krathwohl, D.R., Bloom, B.S. and Masia, B.B. (1964) *Taxonomy of Educational Objectives: The Classification of Educational Goals: Handbook 1: Affective Domain*. David McKay Co.

Krutetskii, V.A. (1977) *The Psychology of Mathematical Ability in Schoolchildren*, (J. Kilpatrick and I. Wirzsup, eds; J. Teller, trans.) University of Chicago Press.

Lappan, G. and Winter, M.J. (1978) "A calculator activity that teaches mathematics," *Arithmetic Teacher*, Vol. 28(7), April

Low Attainers in Mathematics Project (1987) *Better Mathematics: A Curriculum Development Study*. Her Majesty's Stationery Office.

Lumb, D. (1978) "Mathematics for the less gifted: Project report," *Mathematics in School*, Vol. 7(2).

Manitoba Education and Training (1996) *The Common Curriculum Framework for K–12 Mathematics: Western Canadian Protocol for Collaboration in Basic Education*. Winnipeg, Manitoba: Manitoba Education and Training.

Martin, H. (1996) *Multiple Intelligences in the Mathematics Classroom*. Palatine, IL: IRI/Skylight Training and Publishing.

Merrill, M.D., Tennyson, R.D., and Posey, L.O. (1992) *Teaching Concepts: An Instructional Design Guide*, 2nd ed. Englewood Cliffs, NJ: Educational Technology Publications.

Meyer, M. (1997) "Mathematics in context: Opening the gates to mathematics for all at the middle level," *National Association of Secondary School Principals Bulletin*, February 1997, pp. 53–59.

Miller, L.D. (1991) "Writing to learn mathematics," *Mathematics Teacher*, NCTM.

Moghadam, H. and Fagan, J. (1994) *Attention Deficit Disorder: A Concise Source of Information for Parents and Teachers*. Calgary, AB: Detselig Enterprises.

Moore, B.M. (1988) "Achievement on basic math skill for low-performing students: A study of teacher's affect and CAI," *Journal of Experimental Education*, Vol. 57(1).

Moore, G. (1985) "Calculators and remedial education in mathematics," *Remedial Education*, Vol. 20(1).

National Council of Teachers of Mathematics (1986) *Estimation and Mental Computation*. Reston, VA: NCTM.

National Council of Teachers of Mathematics (1989) *Curriculum and Evaluation Standards*. Reston, VA: NCTM.

National Council of Teachers of Mathematics (1991) *Professional Standards for Teaching Mathematics*. Reston, VA: NCTM.

National Council of Teachers of Mathematics (1992) *Calculators in Mathematics Education*. Reston, VA: NCTM.

National Council of Teachers of Mathematics (1993) *Assessment in the Mathematics Classroom*. Reston, VA: NCTM.

National Council of Teachers of Mathematics (1995) *Connecting Mathematics across the Curriculum*. Reston, VA: NCTM.

National Curriculum Council (1989) *Mathematics Non-Statutory Guidance*. NCC.

Neilsen, R. (1995) "Kill All the Calculators?" *Saskatchewan Mathematics Teachers' Society Journal*, Vol. 30/31(3/1).

Nesher, P. and Teubal, E. (1975) "Verbal cues as an interfering factor in verbal problem-solving," *Educational Studies in Mathematics*, Vol. 6.

Open University EM235 Course Team (1982) *Developing Mathematical Thinking*. Open University Press.

Open University PME233 Course Team (1980) *Mathematics Across the Curriculum*. Open University Press.

Pajares, F. and Miller, D. (1994) "Role of self-efficacy and self-concept beliefs in mathematical problem solving: A path analysis," *Journal of Educational Psychology*, Vol. 86(2).

Peel Board of Education Teachers (1996) *Mathematics, Science, and Technology Connections: Activities for Grades 6-9*. Toronto, Canada: Trifolium Books Inc.

Peterson, J.M. (1989) "Tracking students by their supposed ability can derail learning," *American School Board Journal*, Vol. 176(5), p. 38.

Phillips, D.C. (1995) "The good, the bad, and the ugly: The many faces of constructivism," *Educational Researcher*, Vol. 24(7).

Post, T.R. (1988) *Teaching Mathematics in Grades K–8: Research Based Methods*. Boston, MA: Allyn and Bacon, Inc.

Poulter, J.G. and Haylock, D.W. (1988) "Teaching computational estimation," *Mathematics in Schools*, Vol.17(2).

PrIME (Primary Initiatives in Mathematics Education) (1991) *Calculators, Children and Mathematics*. Simon & Schuster.

Robertson, L., Graves, N., and Tuck, P. (1984) "Implementing group work: Issues for teachers and administrators," In N. Davidson (cd.) *Cooperative Learning in Mathematics: A Handbook for Teachers*, pp. 362–379. Menlo Park, CA: Addison-Wesley.

Rosenshine, B. and Meister, C. (1992) "The use of scaffolds for teaching higher-level cognitive strategies," *Educational Leadership*, Vol. 50(8).

Ross, D. (1964) "A description of twenty arithmetic under-achievers," *Arithmetic Teacher*, #11.

Royal Society and Institute of Mathematics and its Applications (1986) *Girls and Mathematics*. The Royal Society.

Saxe, G.B. (1988) "Candy selling and math learning," *Educational Researcher*, Vol. 17(6) (American Educational Research Association).

Schall, W.E. (1990) "Projects for outdoor mathematics," In J. Trowel (ed.) *Projects to Enrich School Mathematics*, pp. 125–133. Reston, VA: National Council of Teachers of Mathematics.

Sewell, B. (1981) *Use of Mathematics by Adults in Daily Life*. Advisory Council for Adult and Continuing Education.

Sutton, S. (1997) "Finding the glory in the struggle: Helping our students thrive when math gets tough," *National Association of Secondary School Principals Bulletin*, February 1997, pp. 43–52.

Tennyson, R. and Park, O. (1980) "Teaching concepts: A review of instructional research literature," *Review of Educational Research*, Vol. 50(1), pp. 50–70.

Thyer, D. and Maggs, J. (1991) *Teaching Mathematics to Young Children*. London, UK: Cassell.

Underhill, B., Uprichard, E., and Heddens, J. (1980) *Diagnosing Mathematical Difficulties*. Charles E. Merrill Publishing Company.

Van De Walle, J.A. (1990) *Elementary School Mathematics: Teaching Developmentally*. New York: Longman.

Weissglass, J. (1984) "Cooperative learning using a small-group laboratory approach," In N. Davidson (ed.) *Cooperative Learning in Mathematics: A Handbook for Teachers*, pp. 295–334. Menlo Park, CA: Addison-Wesley.

Womack, D. (1988) *Developing Mathematical and Scientific Thinking in Young Children*, Special Needs in Ordinary Schools series, London, UK: Cassell.

Index

Note: Information found in tables or sidebars are indicated respectively by a lower case "t" or "n." Names of activities start with capitals.